'24-7' H.R. Guide

for

"Inclusion"

See Books 1&2

www.inclusionPLUSdiversity.com

Gordon Ralph

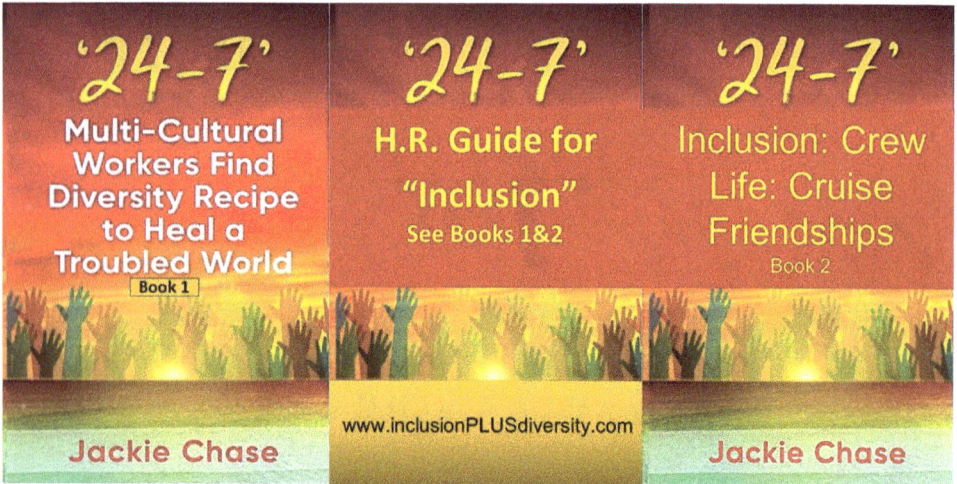

Three eBooks for Worker INCLUSION campaign

'24-7' H.R. Guide for "Inclusion"

See Books 1&2

Gordon Ralph

'24-7' H.R. Guide for "Inclusion" See Books 1&2
Gordon Ralph
www.adventuretravelpress.com, Lady Lake, FL 32159
Copyright © 2019 by Gordon Ralph

'24-7' H.R. Guide for "Inclusion" See Books 1&2
Gordon Ralph
Grayscale Print: ISBN 978-1-937630-48-5
Also available in Color and eBook editions
www.AdventureTravelPress.com

Publisher's Cataloging-In-Publication Data
(Prepared by The Donohue Group, Inc.)

Names: Ralph, Gordon, editor. | Chase, Jackie. '24-7' multi-cul-
    tural workers find diversity recipe to heal a troubled world. |
    Chase, Jackie. '24-7' inclusion.
Title: '24-7' H.R. guide for "Inclusion" : see books 1 & 2 / Gordon
    Ralph, (guide editor).
Other Titles: 24-7 human resources guide for "Inclusion" | Twenty-
    four-seven human resources guide for "Inclusion"
Description: Lady Lake, FL : AdventureTravelPress.com, [2019] | In-
    cludes resources for further reading. | Print version issued
    with either color or black-and-white illustrations. | Guidebook
    issued to support book 1 & 2 of this series.
Identifiers: ISBN 9781937630485 (color print) | ISBN 9781937630447
    (grayscale print) | ISBN 9781937630430 (ebook)
Subjects: LCSH: Diversity in the workplace. | Social integration. |
    Cruise lines--Personnel management. | Tourism--International
    cooperation. | Industrial relations. | LCGFT: Interviews.
Classification: LCC HF5549.5.M5 A12 2019 (print) | LCC HF5549.5.M5
    (ebook) | DDC 658.3008--dc23

'24-7' H.R. Guide for "Inclusion"

See Books 1&2

Ideas on "How to" use eBooks for ALL workers

Audience? **H.R./Leader/Worker who seeks "INCLUSION"**

Goal? **Warm welcoming attitudes/friendships.**

Tools? **eBooks full of worker stories.**

Thanks? **SHRM: key research: "Transformational Diversity."**

Editor? **Publisher@inclusionPLUSdiversity.com**

Invitation? **Read and make history!**

Books 1&2? **Use either or both as gift.**

Measure results? **See options available.**

Hints/ideas? **Soft stories cause imitation.**

Defend effort? **Wide distribution: good defense.**

No downside? **Keep current tactics; nothing lost.**

Readers vicariously travel. **Crew contract not needed.**

"Exclude" some from mailing? **Which ones don't get vaccine?**

Summary of inclusion ideas

Inclusion starts with a friendly attitude by a "host" toward an individual. Eye contact, a smile, and a brief greeting can break the ice. Attitudes are voluntary choices, not controlled by pressure/habits, but by decisions each person chooses in their heart and mind. Good news: people often imitate successful examples.

Diversity could be required/suggested by school admission or hiring quota targets, but friendships can't be forced by legislation or rules. Such strategies would be resisted and counter-productive. Who has a better idea?

Inclusion flourishes where there are conditions in a "friendship laboratory" that can be repeated by other organizations using tools and leadership encouragement.

86 authors: A publisher at www.inclusionPLUSdiversity.com, helped by an internationally prize-awarded author, observed the conditions in one inclusion-successful industry [Hospitality], and interviewed 86 people to describe, in 2 books [about crew on 2 ships], how friendships can be encouraged.

Why experiment without reviewing successful programs in these two "labs"? The tools available to emulate these successes are eBooks full of pictures, fun facts, and anecdotes about the hospitality industry; the books have friendship stories, peer success hints, and a publisher's offer of a free proof-test emailing of the eBooks; this could fine-tune the next mailing: no "exclusions".

The reader can, if desired, choose to put into practice these hints on how to advance in a career and meet interesting friends who are "different" from the reader; this "low key" approach offers a choice, but the ideas are very tempting.

Using eBooks as gifts to ALL workers within organizations is not common, but this tool is a rare and inexpensive opportunity to use an electronic option that has advantages to supplement video or class training. A vaccine for 20% of workers fails; 100% succeeds!

Reading requires learners to pay attention rather than doze or block out the stimulus. It requires the mind to actively process, think about, and internalize the words that are read in order to complete the message loop. Could an idea melt into the reader's life? Books provide time to re-read and absorb.

What is the setting of the "lab"? Book 1 has stories of 35 individuals at one worksite with 2000 crew members [from 79 nations] out of a 77,000-person company, and they work aboard a large cruise ship. Book 2 is about an employer of 2500. There are 51 stories from a 600-person crew representing 27 nations aboard a medium-size cruise ship. Crew interviews are authentic, personal, and persuasive.

Cost? Due to wide distribution, the publisher has lowered the investment hurdle to $2 per book (equal to author royalty obligations) whether emailed or printed, and will waive publisher profits, outlays, or cost-recovery fees.

License? Granted to the organization to customize, translate, print or email whatever number of copies will reach all "includers". [Excluding anyone doesn't achieve the objectives of an inclusive team that treats each contact with fellow workers as family members who joyfully help one another.]

SHRM research laid the foundation for these two eBooks and this "Guide". HR professionals can now view the linkage between hosting a "foreigner" [with numerous differences in language, customs, religion, cultures, foods, gestures and many more] and hosting a person who resides in the same town and culture but happens to have a different gender, skin color, or lifestyle.

The magic? When folks accept the foreign person, even vicariously as a reader, their mind also respects and befriends folks with fewer types of differences. The relevant research is contained in the SHRM book, "Transformational Diversity" [TD] referred to and quoted in the "Guide".

HR professionals are encouraged to see answers to typical objections/questions, within the chapters of Part 1 of this Guide, to test their thinking about how this might help their workers to be "inclusive".

Sample stories. Later parts [4 & 5] include excerpts from the words of workers in each of the interview books covering many related topics.

Fun to read! Color illustrations, interesting format, descriptions of how workers adjust their thoughts to accept strangers from foreign cultures.

Not mere "tolerance of strangers", but celebration of an active curiosity that even leads to an invitation to the stranger's (now friend's) home.

99 to 1 ratio? This Guide suggests the ideal training ratio may be 99% "carrot" [friendship] and less than 1% "stick", [which is the parental standard for good citizenship and not fighting or abusing another worker or guest.] There is zero tolerance of that type of behavior in "Inclusion", but the focus is on friendships.

Top management is invited to write a FOREWORD in customized eBooks, or the organization can use a cover letter that presents the gift as a means to confirm the mission and invite reading.

Proof? There is an option to do a blind study of whether the book changed any minds. Fine industrial psychologists can add a few questions to those designed to check on organization communication and whether the firm is deficient in any area of tools needed for the worker to best complete their mission. What a valuable "annual checkup" of worker attitudes!

Supplement, not replacement. Use eBooks to complement current ideas with practical solutions for each worker or student, reaching all workers at once.

INTRODUCTION: Why not consider a test?

'Inclusion' Guide: Taking Action:

To: HR professional: IF . . .

- *You could test a new tool, free;*
- *And if it worked for dozens;*
- *And it warmed attitudes;*
- *And it worked within days;*
- *And made folks feel "included";*
- *And this Guide explained it all;*
  - o *Would you read it?*
  - o *Would you test it?*
  - o *And include new hires?*
  - o *No one is EXCLUDED?*

Is good attitude worth $2 each [eBook author royalty?]
If print books needed: publisher offers $2 license to
print. eBooks=fun; these stories will warm attitudes.
Please test! You, and SHRM's research, hold the answer.
(SHRM quotes are reprinted by permission).

Inclusion [further thoughts:]
<u>Guide:</u> SHRM Research is the key!

- It started with SHRM's "Transformational Diversity" [TD]
  - The research agrees: "Foreigners" are very "different".
- The good news is they are fun to "host" & befriend.
  - Once attitudes <u>INCLUDE</u> them, other "differences,
    - [Like gender, age, race, religion, lifestyle, etc.]
      - Are OK for friendship per TD guide chapter.
        - Just read Guide for ideas, and act now!

<u>This H.R. Guide & 2 tools [eBooks] are a PACKAGE</u> to help organizations launch a <u>repeatable</u> training addition to their efforts to make <u>every</u> worker/student/new hire feel included, as includer hosts. eBook stories have images & fun quotations.

Combined with strong leadership, a tool distribution could be emailed at same time for all workers, so includers & includees gain new skills for inclusion while refreshing group standards.

<u>Guide presents topics from these 2 "work=family eBooks"</u>, that contain action extracts to be emulated. Extracts save H.R. review time. Similar topics are coded for comparison: eBook is fun to read while employed or recruited.

<u>Formula? NOBODY is excluded</u> from link or email distribution. When inclusive, DIVERSITY happens when worker recruits or supports. <u>SHRM research in TD suggests:</u> [Greeting a "foreign guest": also helps fix gender/race/lifestyle attitudes!] The world's hungry for SHRM-type research and "friend-making" eBooks. Gordon Ralph, Editor; www.inclusionPLUSdiversity.com

Hospitality's an ancient art: eBooks are "how to" for workers:

Book 1: 77,000 worker cruise line: 79 cultures on board
Book 2: 2,500 worker cruise line: 27 cultures on board

eBooks "written" by crew dictation--interviews are authentic;
"Inclusion" is successful: just imitate; no need to re-invent!

SHRM's *"Transformational Diversity"*: Don't "homogenize" differences:
Celebrate them, and make a new friend. The 2 eBooks show how.

See pages 1 to 4 of SHRM book, reprinted in Part 1 by permission: [Copyright
Society for Human Resource Management 2011]
Celebrate, learn, befriend, & enjoy "foreigners";
be a "world traveler/reader!"
Other differences (age, race, gender, lifestyle)
will also then be celebrated.

Organization's leaders have opportunity to lead, encourage, and support
through customized FOREWORD in eBook.

Consider the difference: Most H.R "Inclusion" books tell what the H.R.
specialist <u>must do</u> to change current programs: [Do they work?]. Specific
seminar strategies to reach many workers would have to be bought. They
deploy unevenly over many months: "Includers" & "newbies" trained?
This eBook strategy supplements existing efforts and leaves no one out.

New tools: H.R. leaders can now supplement the strategy of ANY
organization. The eBook tool can be linked, print-copy mailed, or PDF
emailed as gift to reach every worker worldwide within a week. These
tools are fun to read, can be translated to any language, and/or locally
printed for $2 royalty. Specific hints and stories tell the joy of success,
and are not "pushy". They let workers "discover" what makes sense &
makes friends. See multiple clips from both books in Parts 4 & 5 in this
Guide. Test some free eBooks on a representative group of workers,
collect feedback, or measure using industrial psychologists who can
modify a national "wellness" system to evaluate.

<u>*Resource Tool in 8 parts for H.R. professionals:*</u>

Part 1: Key Questions concerning "Inclusion" and how to achieve it.

Part 2: Links to research, theory, and resources by SHRM

Part 3: Brief backgrounds of author and editor/publisher

Part 4: Extracts from Chapters in Book 1 [with topic names index]

Part 5: Extracts from Chapters in Book 2 [with topic names index]

Part 6: Evaluation options and organizational "health" checkup

Part 7: Free trial options: easy steps to achieve Inclusion results

Part 8: Further reading in diversity and inclusion

Foreword

This book highlights several means and benefits of working effectively with a very diverse workforce.

Inclusion Introduction

How to Achieve It with SHRM help
Ideas by Gordon Ralph, Publisher/Editor/Author
Consider:

- The Society for Human Resource Management (SHRM) changed the name of its "Diversity / Inclusion" conference to "Inclusion". Why!
- "Inclusion" is the pleasant action-task of the worker; diversity is the mandated job of the employer. "Inclusion" is hard to quantify; there are new ways to do that.
- Tools for "inclusion" must be effective and affordable, but a top priority is to inculcate friendliness into every worker toward anyone who is "different". Is $2 affordable?
- Tools in this guide include eBooks to consider as a low-cost, effective, attitude change-agent for all workers at a point in time, as described here.
- Inside are numerous links to eBooks on theory. This guide uses modern persuasive tools that can be delivered to every worker electronically or physically.
- It helps when the change-agent story is "written" by interviews of 86 workers themselves who tell stories of exactly **WHAT** they do and **HOW** they befriend others.
- As publisher of these story books, we can customize language for employers willing to share eBooks with their workforce at near-publisher cost for print or eBooks
- The result **WILL BE** an improvement in the bottom line for employers who can now create a team of creative friends that "include" rather than "exclude" their peers.
- The eBooks are fun to read; reading requires active thought-processing and personal involvement, as opposed to hearing speakers or staring at a TV screen and dozing.
- Avoid a WSJ [or legal] accusation of failing to support diversity per a page B1 headline on August 28, 2019 that states, *"Reeling from Criticism, Film Industry Pushes for Diversity".* Send a firm-wide mailing that shows effort.

Part 1: Key Questions concerning "Inclusion" and how to achieve it.

Introduction:

1-_SHRM quotes set the stage with research on pages 1-4 of TD

2-Economic incentives follow respect for fellow workers

3-Brief history of diversity efforts

4-Why is inclusion difficult?

5-Why not do a test in your organization?

6-Resources for workers

7-Inclusion measurement options

8-Language and translations

9-Customizing eBooks

10-Menu for a test mailing

11-Go for the gold (EVERY worker)

12-Thoughts for the future

SHRM quotes set the stage on pages 1-4 of its book "Transformational Diversity"

CHAPTER ONE

The big picture: Employer rewarded; Worker advances

"Why would I want to efriend a ??????"

   This small Guide is about success in bending minds toward INCLUSION! It makes the case for listening to workers who practice that art and who tell their story in an interesting "resort" context so the reader and fellow worker gradually accumulates many examples from 86 interviews, useful every day, by process of inductive reasoning, or seeing many examples that lead to a change in attitude. If a worker has not been exposed to a number of "foreign" people, Books 1 and 2 fill that void with a vicarious cruise.

   One important secret is whether the book is interesting to read. When the setting of the multi-cultural workspace is a large floating resort, it captures the romance of the sea, and it features those who serve guests with happy attitudes. It can be an adult story book with a happy ending, intended to be read (in English or a language the worker understands) by EVERY worker. The wonders of eBook delivery by email or link make that possible, supplemented by printed editions where necessary. Imagine a mass mailing with the potential to modify the attitudes of a hundred or a million workers within a week!

   This Guide includes links to academic and management books with important research and facts, but since workers won't read those, the change agent is actually a book written for them by their peers who are interviewed.

   Why does this work? The author/publisher gives examples within the hospitality industry where this tool of friendly inclusion originates. SHRM, in *"Transformational Diversity,"* establishes that cultural hospitality that welcomes foreign people, who have MANY differences, somehow transfers to less challenging areas like gender and age, where the differences are fewer than those that were just accepted for a wholly different culture.

   Minds are ready to be opened. Several of the books listed herein demonstrate that the attitude of seeing a person as a "stranger" quickly melts, starting with a smile and a simple greeting. The key for a business, charity, government or educational institution is the employee workforce which enables management to take advantage of many efficiencies of running an organization where a user/client/student/worker is king, the reputation for service is second to none, and the acceptance of people who are "different" is prevalent everywhere. An unspoken advantage that employers have is that there are conditions of employment where violations are not tolerated, such as physical fighting or sexual harassment. Though kindness and understanding can't be legislated, their opposites can be forbidden and the results are a climate where natural curiosity and hospitality and smiles can flourish.

Our world is built, starting with the family structure, around the family that then imprints the child with the culture handed down from generations past.

There are "in" groups and "out" groups which could be symbolized by some different species inside a circle. The goal of "inclusion" is to draw that circle around the globe so it **includes** every human and excludes only Martians! We tend to be lazy or thoughtless when we favor "in-group" people who are "just like us", but from experience, we learn that approach is not only boring but destructive. It keeps us from the joy of "travel" which is all about seeing new landscapes and people who would be very interesting to befriend.

Centuries ago, there was legitimate fear that when meeting a stranger in the open, some mischief might occur. Even then, a smile could cause the confrontation to melt and friendships could begin. Try smiling and greeting when you meet someone to test the theory.

But, why would I want to befriend a ?? [Substitute any minority culture, religion, political advocate, or any other "out-group" person who is not "just like me"?] It turns out, when co-workers write the stories about their friendships that started with a smile and a greeting, good things happen. Befriending one of those "?" type persons might not be easy, but it gets easier, and it's good for the career and allows the employer to grow and offer more growth opportunities. And it's fun, because we are all curious and want to know about "foreign" customs, just as we like to take those trips to foreign lands. Sometimes that interesting foreign trip doesn't cost $5,000 in expenses, and two weeks of vacation, but it is inside an interesting book or exists right next door or down the hall.

This doesn't give full credit to the other reasons, besides curiosity, to befriend a "?" Publications mentioned in the appendix under the "Bottom Line" heading tell us that friendly inclusion causes useful creativity and teamwork that has good results in many areas for the employer as well as the employee. In Book 2, there is this quote,

"In 2013 I talked to a friend; we grew up together. He was working with the Cruise Line, and I asked him if he can put me in contact with the agency. [Employee recruiting!]"

The quote would not have occurred with a worker who hated his boss or the company or his peers, because employee recruitment happens only with happy workers.

So, befriending a co-worker who is "different" is a positive for both worker and employer, without even considering the positive atmosphere for problem solving or the financial advantages reported by McKinsey and others in the referenced articles in the appendix. A significant benefit of an interesting book is also the chance to practice learning "English", since in several of the stories told, issues can be misunderstood and friendships are underdeveloped when language skills are weak.

The 4 pages in the SHRM-sponsored book, "TD", suggest that since there are SO MANY differences in a foreign culture (language, customs, race, traditions, religion, lifestyle, and more, the goal of opening minds, when dealing with foreigners is more difficult. But the good news is when the ice is broken, respect, hospitality, and friendship (and sometimes hosting or helping the foreign person), will follow. That celebration of diversity makes inclusion a reality. And it is logical and demonstrable that the easier "differences" that occur within the host nation (e.g. USA or UK) such as gender, age, lifestyle, color, etc. are accepted as a logical extension of the hospitality to the foreign person.

The following four pages from *"Transformational Diversity"* [TD] are reprinted with publisher's permission and with thanks for this valuable foundation for the field work on cruise ships. Those hospitality venues became a successful mind-opening and attitude-bending lab, suggesting that the celebration of friendships overcome many inherited attitudes about ALL differences. The TD analysis implied that there was more work to be done to invent new tools that would put their creative ideas into practice and offer hope that the delicate task of creating enthusiastic and authentic friendships signified inclusion. Welcome to those tools; use them with care and great success. It's worth considering the purchase of TD, a research book, as can be inferred from the first few pages.

It's not too early to suggest that the very speed of the delivery of eBooks is more than just a way to share a thought. Inclusion seminars or eBooks are only effective when completed, so a new hire who bumps into someone without the "coaching" contained in the eBooks could pollute the potential relationship as easily as the recruit who was not given the "school solution" during the hiring or first day encounter with the welcoming committee. That is the REAL reason for getting the word out to EVERYONE at once, so there are no holes in the dike. The publisher thanks SHRM for the privilege they granted us to present, in the next 4 pages, the early goals and breakthrough findings of "Transformational Diversity", which is the foundation for our Books 1 and 2 as tools for positively bending attitudes not only toward new-found foreign friends but to all persons with fewer differences as well. The emphasis (underlined text) is that of the editor of this Guide.

"Chapter 1. Reaching Our Potential with Transformational Diversity

The latest research in diversity, *Global Diversity and Inclusion: Perceptions, Practices and Attitudes,* commissioned from the Economist In-
telligence Unit by the Society for Human Resource Management (SHRM),[1] points out that although North America ranks high for diversity, the potential is far from fulfilled, with the region scoring only
70 out of 100 points. The need to reach our potential is more challenging in our uncertain times. At the same time, organizations need to grow and remain competitive, more so now than ever before. This reality is why the business rationale for transforming diversity and inclusion that we advocate and substantiate in this book rests with synergy-boosting intercultural training for everyone.

In this book we introduce Transformational Diversity® — a new vision of diversity developments that seeks to revise and transform current diversity programs through a strong infusion of an intercultural perspective with intercultural business competencies training. This new brand of diversity is taking the "old" diversity beyond race and gender, proposing the shift of focus from traditional race-gender to minorities-integration-synergy-performance issues. The shift — which

we believe to be of special significance in the time of economic chal
lenges and rapidly changing demographics — needs special attention:
women, as well as U.S.-Americans of color, are regarded as easier to
integrate into corporate cultures (for they share the prevailing national
cultural norms),   while other ethnic minorities and overseas employees
may present more complex issues of cultural backgrounds and styles of
thought. Many business professionals already understand that different demographic groups think and communicate differently, and these
cultural differences need to be understood by all stakeholders — so that
the newcomers to the workplace can be integrated sooner rather than
later. Integration is not easy to achieve, but the expectant prize of an
enhanced bottom line resulting from an inclusive, harmonious, and col-
legial organizational culture is well worth the effort.

   The necessity to complement traditional diversity efforts with con-
sistent, frequent intercultural training that regards national culture as
a key differentiator is validated in the above-mentioned research. The
aforementioned SHRM research report states:

> "As organizations recognize the importance of develop-
> ing greater cross-cultural competence, diversity and inclu-
> sion practitioners are often at the forefront of this work. This
> makes sense, as these professionals have long been engaged in
> helping individuals in ways that allow people from all back-
> grounds to hear and be heard, understand and be understood,
> and work together productively. And some will suggest that
> one's national culture is the most powerful differentiator there
> is, greater than ethnicity, gender or language.[2]

   This thought has been convincingly outlined in recent intercultural research, such as _The Cultural Imperative_ by Richard Lewis, who
explains how some cultural traits are too deeply ingrained to be homog-
enized.[3] Also worth remembering is that presently many established
concepts and approaches are becoming outdated and therefore require
considerable modifications to survive and thrive. Transformational

Diversity, a diversity practice imbued with solid intercultural business competencies training, is inclusive by its nature, and it embraces some best "old" diversity practices (like compliance, affinity groups, and such), but it moves them off center stage as things once necessary but insufficient in today's organizations. It is Transformational Diversity that the nation embattled by change needs.

BACKGROUND

The concept of Transformational Diversity was developed in response to broadly expressed client needs for moving forward while making diversity work more effectively to enhance productivity and performance. The diversity function or discipline of human resources focuses on employee differences as expressed by their experiences, backgrounds, personal qualities, and work style orientations, such as race, age, ethnicity, and disability that can be recognized and used for an organization's business objectives. Inclusion, on the other hand, recognizes that the presence of diversity alone is not a guarantee of success and represents commitment and actionable steps to achieve business benefits; primary among these is a corporate culture that makes people feel respected and welcome.[4] The coupling of inclusion-as-action with diversity developments has been brewing for years,' but now more than ever, diversity should contribute more visibly to productivity and the bottom line to justify its investment. In other words, diversity should change to achieve its full potential.

Transformational Diversity was designed for an increasingly multicultural workplace, which we characterize as the presence and interaction of groups of people of different national and ethnic backgrounds to include their linguistic, socioeconomic, and religious characteristics. In this regard, Transformational Diversity serves as a large umbrella for North American diversity with international interests. It offers powerful potential not only for global but also for pre-global organizations. Transformational Diversity is about a new diversity imperative that transcends traditional diversity and inclusion programming by placing inclusion in the driver's seat. This is the essence of Transformational Diversity. We offer strategic and tactical resources for seamlessly bridging the current diversity inclusion gap and for making diversity globally prepared — within the context of dramatically changing demographics and increasingly multicultural human capital that is in need of appropriate talent development initiatives.

GOALS

We wrote this book with several goals in mind.

First, it will help HR and diversity leaders who may need to reenergize or revisit their work, as we will explain, in light of pressures from increasingly diverse workforce populations to develop globally minded corporate cultures during challenging economic times. We will discuss the main purpose of examining human capital's intercultural competencies initially in Chapter 2 and more substantially in Chapters 3, 4, and 5. This book was written to deliver a call to action in response to domestic diversity practitioners who are struggling to reawaken their efforts in more meaningful directions.

Second, we intended to write the book not only for the "best in class for diversity" companies but for all organizations, big and small, where HR professionals and business leaders are concerned with workforce talent development and productivity. We offer new and different strategies and plans that deal with what is not working in many current diversity programs and what is needed now. The book tackles, foremost, the complex issues of cultural diversity for the benefit of employee engagement.

Finally, we believe that diversity today, to a considerable degree, boils down to its ability to support the organization's ultimate goals of growth and productivity (that is, profitability, market share, innovation, and more) and needs to embrace intercultural understanding of both global and local human capital to achieve those goals. The new incarnation of diversity that we present in this book is pragmatic, practical, and productive — and, also entertaining and exciting with its connection to people's interests in their own professional growth and in putting a new set of skills to work for the good of their organizations. We think of Transformational Diversity as a diversity renaissance totally in sync with modern times."

End of "transformational diversity" quote

CHAPTER TWO

Economic incentives follow respect for fellow workers

"Why would I want to work for ??????

In a tight laor market, one of the more successful options for employers is to let the current workforce know that there is a jo opening with "x" requirements.

If an excellent "inclusion" atmosphere exists, any worker is a likely recruiter for themselves, or a friend or relative with those qualifications. On the contrary, an unhappy worker will not e a word -of-mouth recruiter.

Respect is the magic word. Where it exists in genuine form, it enefits the organization and every individual in it. Books 1 and 2 [See excerpts in Parts 4 & 5] are full of quotes that show how economic incentives, including promotions, follow the presence of teamwork and respect for fellow workers.

Some of the stories evidence a kind of loyalty that would e expected if the person were an owner or partner. Certainly, most employers would love to have workers like these.

Good relationships make the jo more fun, more profitale, and more likely to attract guests or customers so that the usiness expansion is more likely and the potential for advancement will occur faster.

There is even a kind of "team spirit" normally associated with sports teams and regional cheer leading.

Good personal relations and respect for the differences that elong to other cultures seems to have no downside and much upside.

CHAPTER THREE

Brief history of diversity efforts

"Why would I want to associate with employers who hire many "foreigners?"

   This type of thinking may come from growing up with parents who were themselves a part of a local culture without a lot of contact with foreign cultures. The stories in Books 1 & 2 show how quickly and easily friends are made starting with a greeting and a dash of curiosity. Governments egan some years ack encouraging the society aout eing fair to all people, and a long list of human attriutes are officially off limits as reasons to reduce fairness as a result of elongin g to a group on that list.
   There are many ooks full of history lessons aout discrimination ased on irrelevant things when jo readiness standards are considered, ut these days, the emphasis has shifted to the importance of "inclusion" once the hire is complete and there is some diversity among those hired. It's one thing to e invited, ut quite another to e asked to dance, as one spokesperson descries the difference.
   SHRM's ook *"Transformational Diversity"* states that diversity is the state of mind while inclusion is action. It is more important to understand the future, while not minimizing the mistakes of the past. Our thought is that inclusion involves a welcoming that is not forced ut full of joy and authenticity.
   In fact, rather than dwell on all the "don'ts" our ooks 1 and 2 spend their thought time on those joys of friendship and how satisfying they can e. One worker in the ship's shop expressed the initial contact with a stranger as a simple step forward y saying "I just go". In other wor ds, get right to the point and don't make a ig deal out of it. Start talking and words will take care of themselves.
   So, it's not so much aout the history as it is the opportunity of the moment. Looking ack on that moment, it might have started a long friendship or even a visit to a fascinating country that is one of our planet neighors we knew little aout. In that sense, the open mind ecomes educated outside of academic settings and inside of the attitudes of hearts and minds.

CHAPTER FOUR

Why is inclusion difficult?

"Why would I want to include ?????? when it's such hard work?

Is it really hard? The evidence is to the contrary. Almost every quote of actual workers aoard ships (Books 1 & 2   with excerpts here in Parts 4 & 5) involves a positive experience starting with a simple greeting while walking toward a person, with eye contact, and with a smile of welcome and friendliness. That's all there is to it. There is no special effort ut just a general happiness with life and work.

When looking at the efforts made y Human Resources leaders, one would think this is truly hard. For an average person, a smile is not difficult and it tends to make people feel happy themselves. This editor rememers specific days when traveling in an open Jeep in Myanmar (Burma) on dusty roads, and looking at the people walking along the road toward the auto. What was amazing was the reaction to a smile directed toward them that turned on a switch inside their face so it roke into a smile.

It's a universal sign of peace and "all's well". And it was not hard work turning on those smiles.

The hope is that Books 1 & 2 will have enough examples of "how to" so that anyone reading either ook will want to emulate the experience of the story tellers in each chapter. The fun that follows the opening smile will always seem like a worthwhile payment for the effort.

CHAPTER FIVE

Why not do a test in your organization?

"What is the downside of trying out the idea of sharing an eBook with folks?"

Somehow, it's like taking a plunge in a cool swimming pool. You just have to try it, and in fact, the pulisher will work with organizations of any size or type to help them try out the ooks at no cost. So where is the downside? It only requires using contact info that every organization has for its workers, and offering a free ook to them. To make the experience more useful , as others in the organization may wish to evaluate this test, some feedack is eneficial.

The test can evaluate and improve the technical side of getting the ooks to the readers, and we can offer some help there; while documenting a potential change of attitude, the opportunity exists to document other evaluations, such the organization's communication skills and the availaility of resources " health" as well. Call to discuss.

Doing a test is a way to ojectively evaluate the content, technical delivery issues, and the potential for expanding the list to all persons who are stakeholders, including supply chain participants and consultants or, for example, Physicians, who are not actual employees. Anyone in contact with customers or guests could e unfavoraly impacted y a thoughtless or rude person connected to the organization.

If you initiate an inquiry, we will also suggest you look at a couple of industrial testers or psychologists who can help you to ojectively review not only the reaction to the ook as a tool to improve "inclusion" ut the very contact with all the workers opens the chance to evaluate the "climate" and other tools and resources that may need some attention, and this is a very easy way to do this.

We have discussed the fact that this is an area full of sujectivity, and it's never een   easy, so please don't stop whatever else you are doing to help inclusion. Rather consider it a part of the total picture, a "vitamin" to supplement whatever other good things you do to help create a happy atmosphere for worker and guest or client alike.

CHAPTER SIX

Resources for Workers

"Why would workers want to know more?"

Workers are faced with challenges daily. They need to have the tools to solve prolems, and inclusion can e a serious prolem oth on day one after they are hired and, on every day, thereafter. It is natural for them to want all the help they can get. In Book 1 and Book 2, there are many situations that could come up in the lives of workers, and for the most part, the workers were ale to deal with them.

One of the most difficult inclusion challenges involves use of a second language, not the one used y one's parents. Misunderstandings and mistakes can result. Since every worker will receive an eBook to read, many readers will have supervisory responsiilities, and some time shou ld e taken y such supervisors to review the solutions which include patience and cool - headed thinking so as to avoid making matters worse.

When distriuting the ooks, a cover letter from the CEO might include a reference to English, if that is the vehicle for communication, with the suggestion that a different translation might e made availale if requested. Also, the suggestion of remaining patient with misunderstandings or mistakes will tend to make it easier for different Multi-Cultural groups to work together. One of the suggestions y a worker in the two eBook examples is to expect the normal response, and if it is not used, then consider using different words or a translation to clear the issue efore it escalates into a prolem.

CHAPTER SEVEN

Inclusion measurement options

"Why would I want my company to measure such things as organizational re-sources and other comparative measurements against a national average?"

There are ways to measure the vital signs of an organization. These signs are e st documented when workers are assured of anonymity of responses. It turns out that some new measurement tools are availale and the industrial psychologists who devised them are willing to add questions aout the "inclusion" ooks and w hat if any attitudes were changed y them.

This is a special topic where the editor will gladly help, ut would need a request for referral after asking a few asic questions.   There are many other resources, including those availale from SHRM pulications   and conferences, and all we are suggesting is that the occasion for a gloal (every worker) communication might also e a time to take the organization's temperature as a kind of annual health check on areas that might have een overlooked.

Please contact: Pulisher@inclusionPLUSdiversity.com

CHAPTER EIGHT

Language and translations

"Why would a firm consider a translation and customizing?"

The question of language is more important than it may seem. In Book 2, there are several instances where workers gave up on trying to communicate with people who could not converse in English and there was no other common language. One can respect people who can say nothing in a common language, ut there is no meaningful   way to relate to them.

Any gloal organization that expects to operate normally must insist on the aility to communicate in some common language within the segment of the usiness that uses that language.

The pulisher/ editor will grant licenses to translate and reproduce the two ooks meant for improving the feelings of inclusion so that all workers are exposed to those wonderful stories, and no one feels excluded. Just descrie the need and write to Pulisher@inclusionPLUSdiversity.com .

But the other solution should also e ovious. If the ook is interesting, with pictures and trivia to reak up the serious context, then it is a perfect exercise device for workers to practice the common language they are supposed to know, such as English. Several of the 86 interviewees suggested that TV and videos were also helps in practicing their language skills.

CHAPTER NINE

Customizing eBooks

"Why would I want to customize an eBook?"

The answer is simple: ecause you can.   Think of the ully pulpit where the CEO or Board Chairman gets to speak to every worker and other stakehold-ers.

Even just a FOREWORD written with passion to the team could e a shot heard round the world and add weight to the suggestion that the eBook should e thoughtfully read y everyone to get that message   , and the one presented y the content , that asks for respect for all workers to themselves and customers or guests.

If there is some important information that should e in one   or oth of the eBook tools, write to the pulisher requesting the addition of the language and descrie the numer of copies desired for the license and the other terms will e provided. An email to   Pulisher@inclusio_nPLUSdiversity.com will suf-fice.

CHAPTER TEN

Menu for a test mailing

"Why would I want to think aout who is on the test mailing? "

Why not just send to all those with a last name that egins with "A"?   The test mailing could cover cohorts from high to low on the pay scale, and from near and far offices in various nations, and sucontractors not on a payroll, and independent contractors who are consultants, recruiting agents, and people who could act as referrers of potential workers. Then there are the educational institutions where you have employees, ut also students, grant recipients, adjunct faculty and many other stakeholders like medical doctors contracted to work with the hospital.

A test of several functional and income levels might reveal more if done properly, and far away offices may have language and delivery issues to test with a trial mailing.

The list of languages for translations of the ooks might e helpful as well, where English is not suitale.   Survey the language needs and ask for a license the employer could translate into whatever languages are required for "inclusion" of everyone. A very few employers would e shocked to know that this eBook communication tool could e pre -loaded to physical talets or readers that, in volume, might e availale for $30 or so, and other rules or safety material or procedures could e loaded as well. This may have other cost efficiencies for IT and supervisors who could e asked for help with the downloads in some cases. The point is that the test mailing can reveal areas involving delivery not initially known.

CHAPTER ELEVEN

Go for the gold (EVERY worker)

"Why would we not exclude some people from the ook offer? "

Perhaps someone who is on his or her last day might e e xcluded, ut even someone in the hospital may e ored and welcome an email or a link to download a fascinating eBook, so the exclusion list should e very short.

In fact, the list could e extended   to supply chain sucontractors and other stakeholders where a friendliness tool would not e out of place. The very thought of excluding someone from a free ook aout not eing excluded seems izarre.

Begin to think of those stakeholders that may not e d irectly employed. Just within the hospitality industry, think of hospitals and doctors who are not employed directly ut are walking the halls seeing patients from all countries and ackgrounds.

Think of law firms and partnerships and the uilding industry with its contractors and start to think of educational institutions with students from age 14 and up, and professors paid y grants rather than the university. The list for the free ooks   could e extended to many, if this attitude   adjuster were to e made availale   as a good will gesture.

CHAPTER TWELVE

Thoughts for the future

"Why would I want to e concerned aout the future?   "

It turns out that eBooks have not only the capaility of reaching every worker in a short time, ut also of reaching every new hire efore their first day.

This opportunity is greater than would at first e realized. The traditional "Diversity Seminar", with video and discussion, is not likely to e attended y someone whose first day is next week.

Many studies indicate that the feeling of exclusion is strongest on the day of hire, and can remain at peak concern for a while thereafter. In some cases, that "gap" in communication can lead to a cost of as much as 2 times the annual salary due to a misunderstanding originating during onoarding .

For those who are now excited aout lea rning more aout some of the many cultures shared on the planet earth, there are opportunities to travel to remote villages, including hill tries and others living in valleys and mountainous regions and river or jungle environments. There are also vicarious visits availale in the liraries and ookstores in written or video formats.

The author of ooks 1 & 2 has written of her visits around the gloe and her ooks are mentioned in "Author Page" for those interested. Of course, there are dozens of other resources availale, and interested persons will ecome more sensitized and amazed concerning fascinating cultures, handwork, traditions, dances, music, rituals and eyond, so enjoy these exportations and seek out potential friends who have connections to these cultures and villages. In one of the ooks, a crew memer introduces the rest of the crew to Nyepi, a national celeration in Bali that involves a colorful parade designed to clean the atmosphere of unwelcome "spirits"; the parade is followed the next day with total silence and time at home with no cooking or activity that day; indeed, the Bali airport is shut down completely for 24 hours and there are no taxis and no vehicle traffic.

The future could e exciting, or it could   happen that thousands of traditions are lost. Authors are recording traditions that may e overwhelmed y schools and cell phones   and other technology as the old ways from decades past ecome extinct as children give up the crafts and the language of their parents and ancestors. But there are still many enriching opportunities to explore, and sometimes they are as near as a cain ste ward on a ship, or a wait person in a restaurant. Many would love to tell you and their fellow workers aout their culture.

Part 2: Links/resources by SHRM [See Part 8 for additional independently published ones]

Further Reading

The main contriutions to Inclusion offered y this   Guide are the introduction to two eBook tools that will tend to open minds and friendships among workers and customers of organizations. They are fun to read and not threatening or a requirement. They concentrate on the friendship side, skipping the preaching ut including the enjoyment of having a "different" friend.

From a theoretical and academic side, SHRM has partnered with researchers and authors to produce ooks like "Transformational Diversity " that lay the groundwork for these practical "mind changers". But there have een many more ooks for HR professionals than ooks to e read y workers. Some of these professional ooks , for convenience, are listed elow, ut they are seldom suitale for the   workers themselves. They may e helpful to convince the oard and officers of employers that inclusion pays major dividends to the organization. Related resources for top/middle/hopeful managers help create respect for the usiness mission and all stakeholders and are listed with their links. See Part 8 elow.

One of the tools in our "Package" is "'24/7' Multi-Cultural Workers Find Diversity Recipe to Heal a Trouled World" [eBook 1]. Significant quotations from that ook are in Part 4 of this Guide. It   relates personal interview stories that provide examples to every reader showing how important they are to the mission of cultivating a firm's inside and outside relationships. It contains universal ideas they can adapt to any situations including those that involve people from unfamiliar ackgrounds and cultures.

The eBook could e provided without charge to workers y employers. It is also availale without charge y the pulishe   r for a 200-worker test y larger employers.

Likewise, the recent "24-7" ook,   [eBook 2] has the same pattern of interviews, ut on a smaller ship,   so the worker is again sharing personal solutions with the reader. If there are other such employee interview ooks that we have not listed, please contact the pulisher, as   we can update the eBooks and add the listing quite easily.

The following ook titles can e ordered   from SHRM ut processed through Amazon and are primarily intended for managers of an organization, ut those in the ranks who wish to add skills or clim t he success ladder may also wish to peruse one or more of the titles. The ooks approach the topic of improving organizational culture, often analytically, in ways different from the informal stories for a general population in "24-7", series of ooks.

The www.InclusionPLUSdiversity.com and the www.AdventureTravelPress.com wesites, will add new ooks, editorially sifted [selected] y relevant diversity criteria applied here. In ooks 1 & 2, all organizations can access a variety of tools, warmly shared y words of crew memers, to ridge cultural diversity, gender, age and   other differences and accomplish great missions, all packaged in a "ready to email" format to e read y all employees.

In the following pages, a numer of ooks are listed, in the spirit of "fair use" honoring those chosen with links to the supplier, expanding the toolkit into helpful areas for company managers, new, experienced, or hopeful. Any reviews are listed for convenience and are not the opinions of this pulisher or editor.

Comments of any kind can e directed to the pulisher y email at: Pulisher@InclusionPLUSdiversity.com

SHRM ook listing links contain the title, and click link to access them:

https://store.shrm.org/Transformational-Diversity-Why-and-How-Intercultural-Competencies-Can-Help-Organizations-to-Survi

https://store.shrm.org/Lions-and-Tigers-and-Bears-Oh-My-A-Parable-on-Diversity-and-Inclusion

https://store.shrm.org/Measuring-Diversity-Results-Vol.-One

https://store.shrm.org/The-Diversity-Scorecard-Improving-Human-Performance

https://store.shrm.org/Making-Diversity-Work-Seven-Steps-for-Defeating-Bias-in-the-Workplace

https://store.shrm.org/Without-Excuses

https://store.shrm.org/How-Women-Mean-Business-A-Step-by-Step-Guide-to-Profiting-from-Gender-Balanced-Business

https://store.shrm.org/Why-Women-Mean-Business-Understanding-the-Emergence-of-our-next-Economic-Revolution

https://store.shrm.org/The-Next-Generation-of-Women-Leaders-What-You-Need-to-Lead-but-Wont-Learn-in-Business-School

https://store.shrm.org/Lean-In-Women-Work-and-the-Will-to-Lead

https://store.shrm.org/Diversity-Training-ROI-How-to-Measure-the-Return-on-Investment-of-Diversity-Training-Initiatives

https://store.shrm.org/Shock-of-Gray-The-Aging-of-the-Worlds-Population-and-How-it-Pits-Young-Against-Old-Child-Agains

https://store.shrm.org/24-7-Multi-Cultural-Workers-Find-Diversity-Recipe-to-Heal-a-Troubled-World

https://store.shrm.org/Measuring-Diversity-ResultsBk-Software

https://store.shrm.org/Harassment-and-Diversity-Respecting-Differences-Employee-Manager-DVD-Combo

https://store.shrm.org/Harassment-and-Diversity-Respecting-Differences-Employee-Manager-DVD-Combo

https://store.shrm.org/Overcoming-Bias-Building-Authentic-Relationships-across-Differences

https://store.shrm.org/Managing-the-Older-Worker-How-to-Prepare-for-the-New-Organizational-Order

https://store.shrm.org/WE-Men-Women-and-the-Decisive-Formula-for-Winning-at-Work

https://store.shrm.org/Winning-the-War-for-Talent-in-Emerging-Markets-Why-Women-Are-the-Solution

https://store.shrm.org/What-If-Short-Stories-to-Spark-Diversity-Dialogue

https://store.shrm.org/Trailblazers-How-Top-Business-Leaders-are-Accelerating-Results-through-Inclusion-and-Diversity

https://store.shrm.org/The-Girls-Guide-to-Being-a-Boss-Without-Being-a-Bitch-Valuable-Lessons-Smart-Suggestions-and

https://store.shrm.org/Diverse-Teams-at-Work-Capitalizing-on-the-Power-of-Diversity

https://store.shrm.org/Trainers-Diversity-Source-Book.-Book-CD-ROM-HR-Source-Book-series

https://store.shrm.org/Diversity-Mosaic-Participants-Wkbk.-Dev.

https://store.shrm.org/The-Diversity-Discipline-Implementing-Diversity-Work-with-a-Strategy-Structure-and-ROI-Measureme

https://store.shrm.org/The-Cultural-Fit-Factor-Creating-an-Employment-Brand-That-Attracts-Retains-and-Repels-the-Right

Part 3: Brief background of author and editor/publisher

Author, and Photo-Journalist, Jackie Chase has earned some 33 international book contest awards for over 20 books written in the past 5 years about many aspects of travel to remote parts of the globe. The books feature tribal scenes, stories, and customs and are profusely sprinkled with story-telling photos. For example, her *"100 People to Meet Before You Die"* anthology of adventures in 12 countries and many villages has 321 such stunning photos. She can be reached, through www.CulturesOfTheWorld.com and JackieChase.com.

Her two books in the "24-7" series are about a large and a smaller cruise ship, where the interviews of crew spanned several weeks for the first and some 4 months for the second book. The intention was to have the reader feel connected to each story so, without the cost and time of travel, each reader could step into the crew member's mind and heart and deal with new friendships from around the globe. View the web page for her books at: www.inclusionPLUSdiversity.com.

Publisher and editor, Gordon Ralph has recognized the teaching potential of the hospitality industry, because their workers and their guests represent many of the major cultures of the world. In a setting that is romantic, on the Allure of the Seas, one the world's largest floating resorts, some 79 nationalities are aboard, and 35 of them share their stories in '24-7'. In addition, 27 cultures were on the other ship where 51 workers were interviewed.

His career has involved a year on the Law School Faculty at the University of Chicago Law School studying the interaction among genders, races, backgrounds and ethnicities as project design member and on-site recorder for a history-making study of jurors' attitudes and opinion changes from before and after mock trials. It was sponsored by a grant from the Ford Foundation.

After his Law Review work as an Editor, and his graduation, he did many pro bono projects, such as being Founder of Literacy Services of WI, where some 31.000 have since received tutoring without charge to obtain GED credits and learn English as a second language over the past decades. In addition, he joined Dr. Frank Laubach in Kenya to launch a national literacy campaign in 11 tribal language areas. Dr. Laubach, the "Each One Teach One" President of Laubach Literacy helped tribal peoples to read and write in their 312 languages in over 100 countries. Gordon's volunteer work led to his establishment of Manpower Teaching Services as a contract provider of literacy and ESL language tutoring to many major companies in some 20 states (AT&T, Montgomery Ward, etc.) contracted by employers to help upward mobility for workers who needed coaching in English language and literacy skills.

His current dream is to have every academic and business organization share story books with their workforce and students showing that it's fun and profitable to open arms to people with all kinds of backgrounds, skills, and fascinating stories. The two eBooks he has edited from the cruises are a non-threatening tool that could, with kindness and vision, help open minds and hearts to the magnificent and interesting variety of team members who populate our organizations.

Part 4: Extracts from Chapters in Book 1 [with topic names index]

Book 1: '24-7' Multi-Cultural Workers Find Diversity Recipe to Heal a Troubled World.

These stories flow from the mouths of a ship's crew, sharing with the interviewer a behind-the-scenes look at secrets that create the magic of cruising. They tell about the special lives of crew members and what it feels like to be on a team with folks from seventy-nine cultures. Hidden within each story, there are some gems, highlighted in purple text, (a blend of red and blue). These crew stories could impact our lives at work and play; they offer hope for a future world where we might discover the truth that each of us has a special role as we live together in a house called earth. The reader may, like crew members, celebrate, and learn from, our differences and contributions, while making a friend.

We may learn that even though we might have grown up in different cultures, we are still part of a large human family. We can polish the gems gleaned from these pages, learn about the other members of our world family, and respect them. The author, Jackie Chase, has traveled to over 100 of the world's cultures, often primitive ones, and has observed what all of us have in common. Her five major books have together garnered over 30 awards and stimulated our desire to understand our human similarities and differences. Today's cruise ships show how crew members (like these from 79 cultures) work together in a confined space for months at a time and act as a team.

The story of respect for our world's many cultures started centuries ago at the dawn of religion. Ethics rules developed as humankind wrestled with the similarities and differences they observed in contacts with other people. The family played a strong role in forming a protection for its members, and families grew into tribes, and tribes into villages, and villages into nations. The language-barrier hurdle, plus fear and the survival instinct, contributed to friction among groups. Sometimes, religious passions seem to hurt, rather than help, tolerance and friendship. Modern western nations have adopted various rules to outlaw discrimination based on a long list of human attributes and associations, such as gender, race, religion, and a much longer set of conditions.

The book emphasizes the stories of how a variety of people, representing many of those attributes and childhood experiences, have come together by the hundreds to live and work together in a marine environment the width of a couple of city lots. These workers must rely on each other's sincere cooperation, and even friendship, to carry out the mission of the cruise line: to please the guests. Though these interviews tell the tale of just one such ship at one point in time, the stories can represent imitation opportunities at any hotel, resort, business, charity, or government agency. In a world fraught with local, regional, and national conflicts, the small miracle of a well-managed cruise ship deserves a second look, for it seems that anything worthwhile requires thought, planning, execution, and maintenance of set standards. The people seem to have met the test. The author looked at this, not from a scientific or academic view, but rather as a reporter, sharing with readers some candid observations. This employer has challenged the earth's communities of employers, cities, and nations to take the lessons to heart and apply the "ten-foot-rule" [explained in the book] to daily lives.

The stories shared with the author detail a variety of backgrounds of the people who have found joy in the common mission of pleasing guests. Blended with great ships, delicious food, elegant staterooms, diverting activities, and breathtaking destinations, the addition of staff from all around the globe frosts the cake and fills a guest's memories with that unique and special cultural extra that brings them back for more cruising adventures while enriching their lives. The book emphasizes crew stories about the mission of the employer from the business and entertainment side of managing and running a resort on water. All workers associated with this cruise line or any other employer that encourages multi-cultural respect should feel great pride in being associated with such an organization. Each reader, guest, manager, student, or employee, as stories unfold, can absorb, and imitate the ideas and perhaps change a life or organization, possibly their own.

The interview stories below are substantially in the words of the workers; they have universal application and appeal, not only to show HOW to relate so as to include all persons, but to share the context of work and family in that joyful task of making friends and satisfying our human need to learn and communicate.

The format is one that organizes each person's words as they touch on different ways to share the wisdom of two examples in the hospitality industry that actually work. No need to reinvent a solution for good business and good friendships. Book One is excerpts from 24-7, {biggest ship afloat at the time] and Book Two contains interview language from Crew Life, [smaller ship], both by award-winning author Jackie Chase. Publisher Gordon Ralph, the compiler of these useful-to-workplace word tools was present as a co-interviewer at all interviews contained in both books. The goal was to have a fun-to-read tool available for distribution by H.R. or top management, where it speaks for itself if distributed to every worker (or student) so the welcoming attitude is potentially present everywhere. Worker-to-worker works!

Chapter

eBookskeyed topicsBook1

Book	Last# Chapter	Last # Topic	[# after letter = total# of quotes]	
B1	C22	A4	B1-C22-A4: Age/Gender	A
B1	C34	C4	B1-C34-C4: Creativity	C
B1	C23	D3	B1-C23-D3: Development	D
B1	C31	E10	B1-C31-E10: English	E
B1	C32	F8	B1-C32-F8: Friendliness	F
B1	C32	G20	B1-C32-G20: Guests	G
B1	C5	H2	B1-C5-H2: Heart/Hugs/Habits	H
B1	C23	K3	B1-C23-K3: Kindness	K
B1	C31	L9	B1-C31-L9: Leadership	L
B1	C35	M16	B1-C35-M16: Multi-cultural	M
B1	C9	N2	B1-C9-N2: Nationalities	N
B1	C30	O2	B1-C30-O2: Opening up	O
B1	C25	R6	B1-C25-R6: Respect	R
B1	C33	T10	B1-C33-T10: Team/Family	T
B1	C31	U4	B1-C31-U4: United Nations	U
B1	C23	V3	B1-C23-V3: Visiting	V
B1	C27	W1	B1-C27-W1: Workers	W
B1	C4	Y1	B1-C4-Y1: Youth	Y

Quotes below are from interviews of crew members. Collectively these are worker's tips.
Key to Codes: Book/Chapter/Topic; number after topic letter is order of book appearance.

CHAPTER ONE: Captain: *Being at sea is an obsession.*

B1-C1-R1: Respect: Never out of place. If you treat people with respect, you receive respect in return.

B1-C1-C1: Creativity: A big bowl is best: This is wonderful, compared to working with one nationality. The advantage is that you have a different way of thinking, and you are not the stereotype. If you were a group of Norwegians, you would know how each would react, and the result might be that there is only one way to do something without question. That goes for all nationalities, whether American, Filipino, or Jamaican. To get all these ideas into a big bowl and then review how to do things is what makes our product so unique."

B1-C1-E1: English: Communication is the key. Effective communication with different cultures challenges the best of us. Rules about proper behavior affect verbal and non-verbal communication. Cultures provide people with specific ways of thinking, seeing, hearing, and interpreting their worlds. I think one of the things I was very impressed with was the equal opportunity that was given to each and every person, so you had the opportunity to grow. It's only you, yourself, who needs to put that initiative there.

CHAPTER TWO: Inventory Manager. *Supplies when needed*

B1-C2-G1: Guests: Meeting guests' expectations. When a person leaves this ship, they leave with a smile," says David. "Because in each country the cultures are so different, what might be good for you might not be good for me. A controlled cultural diversity class allows all team members to understand all ways of expression. Working on the same common goal of meeting the guests' expectations becomes easier with everyone understanding each other."

B1-C2-K1: Kindness: Cabin togetherness. So now, we have everybody understanding each other and all working for the same common goal: to meet the guests' expectations. Because the crew members spend so much time together, they become an extended family, a part of each other. Respect tells the whole story. When sharing a cabin with another, the first person a crew member sees when he wakes is his cabin mate. Helping that person creates a unique togetherness for an unbeatable operation.

B1-C2-D1: Development: Different when you leave. He says, "It is the culture of the ship. People think you are forced to do this, but it's not so. It's genuine love for what you do. You may come on board the ship, not as a waiter but to handle luggage or polish woodwork, and you get into service areas and you've developed into this person who genuinely cares. And you are becoming a better person. You come in one way, and you leave another."

B1-C2-G2: Guests: Meeting You change; guests are happy. The only way to make guests happy is to change and be receptive to change. I have to do everything within myself to come to work, smile, and create an environment that is workable, happy, so that our people are happy, and this transfers from you to the guest.

B1-C2-L1: Leadership: The crew must be happy. I can say with conviction, there is no company in the world that can say the same, that we have done so much to ensure happiness for our thousands of employees, whether ship board or shore side, since we started the company. We have great leaders. I think it is their conviction that the crew must be happy. The crew is the backbone of this organization. The crew is what makes it happen.

CHAPTER THREE: Information technology. *Fix that bug.*

B1-C3-E2: English: Crew helps with English. For her, motivation comes from her team, which invests both energy and training in helping her reach her goals. Although the crew speaks English for cruise ship work, the accents of different nationalities make it difficult to understand her fellow crew at times. Eager to assist, team members play an active role in assisting others with language difficulties.

B1-C3-G2: Guests: Satisfied guests. She shared wonderful feelings of receiving a Christmas card each year from a satisfied guest she met one day on a cruise. She says, "Whether at home or on the ship, you have to make [the experience] the best by saying, beyond fear, that you are proud. I am traveling, and now my new friends at sea are family.

CHAPTER FOUR: **Assistant Manager, Children's area.** *Non-stop memory making for kids*

B1-C4-E3: English: Everybody's equal. Only three percent of the crew are Americans, putting me in the minority. And of the first thirty friends I made on ship, none of them were Americans. On ships, you would think there would be a separation, but there is not. You look at someone's nametag just to wonder where are you from; what's your name? But it just gets blown out the window. Accents even get blown out the window. When you are home it's like where is that (accent) coming from? Here, you never hear the same accent. You get used to it instantly, and it's nice because it is a cultural melting pot, with the freedom of knowing that no one is judging other cultures, and that everyone has a voice. Good captains make the crew feel that everyone has a similar voice, whether you have three stripes or work in the galley. Here, you know, is one of the few places I've been in the world where there isn't that judgment.

B1-C4-M1: Multi-Cultural: Everybody's equal. It's as if you were to bring a cultural melting pot together in different scenarios. Here, the crew has to live, work, eat, sleep, and do everything together so everyone has to adapt to each other's cultures. And, what other job allows you to meet 6,000 new guests every single week?"

B1-C4-N1: Nationalities: Old friends aren't culturally prepared. With kids, it's a group function. They don't need to know each other's language. They all find comfort and commonality in that activity. Whether or not they speak the same language or have different skin tones gets lost the second they start turning to games. It's refreshing. I know a lot of friends I grew up with are not culturally prepared, and they come visit me on a ship, and they get a little overwhelmed going to the mess and meeting a bunch of Filipinos or a bunch of people from Trinidad.

B1-C4-H1: Heart/Hugs/Habits. What is too close for comfort? Each culture has different standards for closeness and personal space, and the staff keeps this in mind when problems arise among the children based on these differences.

B1-C4-Y1: Youth: A joy to learn. What a pattern for the world to emulate as the next generation learns the joy of inter-cultural contacts and understanding.

CHAPTER FIVE: Production Manager: *The show floats on*

B1-C5-H2: Heart/Hugs/Habits: Eating habits are different. I remember the second night on board the ship, I was sitting in the crew mess and on one side somebody was eating fish heads and on the other they were eating pig's feet

B1-C5-E4: English: English: sort of. Everybody speaks English one way or another. Most of the electricians who work for me are Croatian. It took me a little time to adapt to the language but you get used to how they ask for things, how they say things. Yes, they'll [digress] into their own language, but I just go with it, and then they break down what they're saying to your level [of understanding]. They don't baffle you with science. It's quite amazing how everybody will just pull together and sort things out.

B1-C5-C2: Creativity: Everybody gets flexible. Adaptability: the middle name for managers and crew members alike. For those newbies who show signs of a closed-minded attitude, the motto of those more experienced is just to show them the right way, how to adjust.

CHAPTER SIX: Executive Housekeeper. *Get all your friends together.*

B1-C6-M2: Multi-Cultural: Doors open. Meeting people of so many nationalities, he experienced doors opening all around the world.

B1-C6-R2: Respect: Challenges work: usually. Accepting that you have to do the same training over and over again, with different nationalities coming in with unique ways of doing things, closes the gap between you and them. You build up some great friendships and, unfortunately, at times, you have to let go of some. Don't take things personally as the other person may not have meant it that way."

B1-C6-T1: Team/Family: Friendly rivalries. When you have a greater mix of nationalities, people tend to come out of themselves and push each other to achieve. If you work in your comfort zone with your *paisanos* (as we call our fellow countrymen, or good friends) on ship, then you tend to relax because they will support you and even help with your work duties. Diversity creates competition or friendly rivalry.

B1-C6-G4: Guests: They like to meet other cultures. People come to cruise lines from around the world to enjoy a getaway. Guests appreciate a cruise ship with crew members representing seventy-nine nationalities because this offers those foreign guests the opportunity to speak with someone using their own language and makes following directions to the library or a quiet place to sit and have a glass of wine a lot easier.

CHAPTER SEVEN: Landscape Specialist: *Into your back yard.*

B1-C7-G5: Guests: A relaxing thought. Imagine a day where you visit with people from many cultures, or sip a beverage of choice just outside of a gourmet restaurant, while watching birds, butterflies, and exotic plants in the middle of the ocean as you delight to a live concert featuring a Brahms trio softly blending with your conversation.

CHAPTER EIGHT: HR Officer: *Celebrate Diversity*

B1-C8-L2: Leadership: What about values? Training managers understand the dynamics of cultural diversity and problem-solving techniques. Several training managers will work onboard, executing the training along with the safety officer, security officer, and environmental officer. The training and development managers focus predominantly on values, ethics, new hires, leadership training, cultural diversity, and other organizational needs.

B1-C8-U1: United Nations: The world learns. The world can learn from this work schedule and integration, especially the United Nations! Here, none of life's issues divide into black or white, good or bad, in or out. Cultural traits and customs, deeply embedded in people from birth, provide myriad ways of thinking, seeing, and hearing.

B1-C8-E5: English [Gestures]: Non-verbal culture answers: Movements of the hands, face, or body, convey very different meanings depending on social or cultural settings. The significance of the same gesture could range from complimentary to highly offensive in different countries. The smile, the most common facial expression in the world, can give conflicting messages depending on which nationality gives or receives it. Russians consider a smile, given freely to strangers (as we Americans do), as impolite or strange. In Asia, a smile can signify embarrassment, while the Scandinavians consider showing emotion, like a smile, as a weakness. Imagine the confusion when a crew member from Bulgaria or the Middle East moves his head up and down as to signal "no" while smiling. The rest of the world uses that movement to signal yes! Connecting the thumb and forefinger in a circle and holding the other fingers straight signals "okay" or "everything's fine" for most of the world, but not if one lives in Iran or certain parts of Latin America where that sign is offensive.

B1-C8-E6: English [Gestures]: Private space cautions: Touching, hugging, kissing on the cheeks, or even touching the head of a child, could signal a violation of one's private space in some societies. Nonverbal communication includes the use of physical space. Both Americans and Europeans demand more space to satisfy their comfort levels than Middle Easterners or Latin Americans. The latter might ask, "Why do you stand so far from me?" The former might ask, "Why do you stand so close?" One of the more noticeable differences between nationalities, with nonverbal communication occurring 'round the clock, is eye contact. Latin Americans and Americans consider not looking someone in the eye as suspicious or disrespectful behavior. Yet, prolonged eye contact in some Asian countries symbolizes disrespect. Learning in advance about cultures and methods of nonverbal communication can save one embarrassment and many misunderstandings.

B1-C8-E7: English: [Hiring]-Not a problem. Hiring problems? Despite having seventy-nine nationalities, that is not really an obstacle. It might take some people a little longer to grasp something, certainly when you are relaying information about how critical it is to work together as we all do in this world, as well as with acronyms and that kind of thing. I think because people work and live together, there is a lot of interaction between individuals, so they get to know each other very quickly and they are incredibly accepting of each other.

B1-C8-M3: Multi-Cultural: It works well. It would be naive of me to bring everybody in and believe everybody will be happy. You will have people who don't adapt to the environment and they move on. But, by and large, the greater majority does get along. The common denominator is they want to work here. Because we do the training, understanding diversity even in all our own interactions, we never focus on slanting something in a particular direction. "We celebrate diversity. And it is an inclusive environment.

B1-C8-A1: Age-Gender: Getting along with differences. Honestly, you might venture into the social norms, but that would be more like how men approach women or women approach men. Here it is concentrated. They are together all day and all night. She summarized the guest situation this way. Many guests sail on a specific ship because a crew member offers such remarkable service. Countless letters arrive describing the level of service a crew member extended during a guest's visit. Crew members extending that courtesy become a part of those guests' lives. This dedicated crew member accepts the rhythm of the assignment and takes pride in this "universal" culture welded into a team from many nations on board.

<u>CHAPTER NINE: Executive Housekeeper: *Help somebody*</u>

B1-C9-N2: Nationalities: A relaxed but disciplined workplace. Training "We are one family. It is so rewarding at the end of the day to ensure that everybody is looking in the same direction. It is challenging at certain points because we do have different nationalities. The policies and the procedures that are in place to ensure that there are very high levels of respect among the crew members is something unique. We have zero tolerance toward disrespect and to offensive behavior. Everybody brings a piece of experience, contributes to the team, and that makes it a diversified team. And when you apply a management style, you can gain so many different visions and ideas and then incorporate them, mix them up, then shape them and achieve great results."

B1-C9-G6: Guests: Please the guest. Training is key. We are the personal assistants of our guests. We are ensuring that everybody is feeling comfortable in his or her home away from home.

B1-C9-G7: Guests: A choice eliminates complaints. He commented: We cannot help everyone to be so open-minded to different foods and experiences. But it is great that we have all those choices, and at the end of the day, everyone can go ahead and experience different options.

B1-C9-G8: Guests: A sense of humor. Many guests choose to leave their luggage outside their stateroom door on the last night of cruise, so the staff can deliver it to the port, and the guest doesn't have to carry it ashore. Late on the last cruise night, a careful wife packed the suitcase to leave outside their door with all her husband's clothes. When he awoke, the suitcase was loaded on huge pallets and on its way ashore so his choice for clothing was towels or nothing. He chose towels. I hope that he went home with a smile.

B1-C9-D2: Development: Changes happen. Working on a cruise ship changes a person. Not only will you become well-rounded and worldly, but you will come away with a better understanding of global problems, and the culture and way of life of people from around the globe.

CHAPTER TEN: Environmental Officer: *Consumers don't see waste*

B1-C10-L3: Leadership: Sofa and cats. Raising two teenagers, two dogs, and two cats, this sailor finds the sofa a popular place back home. Growing up with a ship captain for a father, his life revolved around ex-pats from the far corners of the world. Clean oceans and beaches are an essential part of the cruise experience. Just as important is the protection of sensitive marine habits and wildlife. The cruise industry has a stake in protecting the ocean environment. New technologies help minimize the environmental impact from cruise ships.

CHAPTER ELEVEN: Activities Manager: *Seeing Walmart for first time*

B1-C11-F1: Friendliness: Adjustment made easy. Life at sea perfects life skills starting with the "ten-foot policy." If you are ten feet away from a person, you acknowledge them with a smile; at a distance of four feet, you greet them. A simple 'good morning,' 'good afternoon,' or 'lovely day' makes for a beautiful environment. Smiling is habit-forming. When walking down the street while on vacation, and off the boat, a crew member putting the ten-foot policy to work catches strangers by surprise. Land people are not used to such friendliness, but the response is always positive.

B1-C11-T2: Team/Family: It works both places. His mother has learned all about the ship. She's applied the ten-foot policy to her hairdresser business. Even in the small details, like serving tea and cakes, she has seen a difference in her profitability and clientele. He has told his mother, If I ever find myself making business on land, then ninety-five percent of that business knowledge I will have learned aboard the ship.

B1-C11-G9: Guests: A relaxing Training For me, life is a cycle, with small ones and big ones [experiences]. Once you realize this, you do your best job, the people get happy, and you get happy, and the ratings [customer reviews at the end of the cruise week] are good. The guests have more enthusiasm when they approach the activities on the ship, which means they give you more energy as a host, meaning you have more fun and can do a better job, and the cycle just gets bigger and bigger [people being happy].

B1-C11-F2: Friendliness: We have the software: People! We have the world's largest cruise ship, and we have the best hardware, like the LED screens in the Aqua-theatre. Now we need the software to match, and that is the staff, and the way they approach the situations, how they host activities, and manage them.

So that is my driving force. That's what I love about us and wish the earth and the world could take more of a stand like that, but obviously, we can't fire you from your life. Effective communication comes with time.

B1-C11-T3: Team/Family: Home is where you make it. Tell a Polish, Jamaican, or Indian person that the sky is blue and all will perceive the idea in a different way. Nationalities respond differently to coaching and communication, which gives the managers the responsibility of determining who have the stronger personalities versus the timid crew needing a little more tender hand holding. Land people have more interaction with their families than crew members. But, when crew members return home, they may find a sister who lives above her parents in a duplex and only sees those parents once a month, perhaps when coming or going to work. At the same time, the crew member spends so much time with his/her parents, they can get annoyed at times.

B1-C11-F3: Friendliness: Food for thought. He misses the spontaneous breakfasts, lunches, and dinners in the mess hall. They have these big round tables that seat eight, and I always sit at one of those because I need more space and I am always busy working, and because I know people are going to sit down who have different nationalities. And the part I love the most is you always can speak to somebody. There will be at least three different cultures from around the world that you can have a meal with.

CHAPTER TWELVE: Guest Services Manager: *We are more fragile away from home*

B1-C12-F4: Friendliness: It's a habit. The challenges of ship life that crew members experience can feel overwhelming to them, but their comfortable environment helps them cope. One hundred percent of the crew members who pass along the long corridor that goes from the bow to the stern on deck two, (affectionately called "I-95" by all the employees), will smile. Projecting yourself as available for every situation that comes along helps you do your best to assist.

B1-C12-V1: Visiting: What an opportunity to see a home. Meeting people from all over the world creates a bond that often results in crew opening their homes to one another. Invitations to home countries allow intimate relationships to build between crew members who then have a better understanding of that part of the world.

CHAPTER THIRTEEN: Executive Chef: *Soup's on*

B1-C13-E8: English: Communication is fascinating. Every nationality is great to work with. You learn a little more about that country. Let's say Asian people never say no to you. It's a matter of respect. Then the Caribbean people, just the way they talk, you understand, it's a free style of life. You see Indian people, they make this gesture to you, and it actually means I am listening to you. At the beginning, you think it makes you crazy or makes you feel crazy, if you communicate in all their ways of communication.

B1-C13-M4: Multi-cultural: Choices. I am always amazed over the years because all the HR [Human Resources] issues come to me about the people who have problems with different nationalities. I never had them. In fact, if you put two Jamaicans in the same cabin, then it's the same issues. I would rather have somebody from a different nationality in my cabin because I think it's nice to know more. I have 350 employees.

CHAPTER FOURTEEN: Casino Hostess: *Self-described vampires*

B1-C14-M5: Multi-cultural: Tread cautiously with some issues. Regarding the cultural diversity of the crew members and the guests, she commented on issues that could arise over politics, sports, or religion. She said that focusing on the job and encouraging teamwork, help alleviate interpersonal conflict with every new encounter. Politics and religion become a moot point and never an issue.

CHAPTER FIFTEEN: Facilities Cleaning Manager. *Ship shape*

B1-C15-R3: Respect: Necessity is the mother of cooperation. Living in a small cabin with a stranger who isn't sensitive to your cultural background stirs the emotions. Quickly cabin mates learn flexibility. With new adjustments comes new knowledge about another culture and its customs. Sometimes, even between people from the same country, personalities just don't mesh, and talks with managers help resolve such issues. Management does its best to honor request forms for change of roommates.

CHAPTER SIXTEEN: Hotel Director: *Let's float a resort*

B1-C16-M6: Multi-cultural: Choices hospitality industry. We are in a business where you provide great service to people and make them feel comfortable. I think anybody who doesn't like people should not go into this kind of professional environment. I think they should repair cars or do something else more suitable. There is no high pressure here. It is a lifestyle. What really separates ships and jobs on land is that here your job and your life are interconnected. Not your life as a whole, but your day-to-day life. Whereas on land you finish your job and go home.

B1-C16-M7: Multi-cultural: Get the job done. I don't worry about how many hours I work. I worry about getting the job done and taking care of every detail. So, my heart changed here with this job. It doesn't matter where my colleagues come from, especially those who are in this lifestyle for a while. We all agreed that we'd become world-wise, and we are far more open-minded than other people who have never left home.

B1-C16-M8: Multi-cultural: Why am I here? "People are here for a couple of purposes. Some want to see the world when they are young, but then when they are here for more than two years, they customize the idea because of the income and security, seeing a career opportunity. I am Austrian and there are young people at home who don't have a job they want, and I am trying to tell them, why don't you go out in the world? I mean, you have education. Say to yourself I am going to do something else for a few years. There is, I don't know, a hesitation or reluctance because they hear different sides, like the income is not good, or I don't want to leave my family, or I don't want to stay here so long. I think in today's world in many cultures, especially the economically successful cultures, I am talking Central Europe and Northern America where the economies and the social nets are strong, people are less inclined to be adventurous and take opportunities.

B1-C16-M9: Multi-cultural: Choices. The training emphasized the international flavor of things, the blending of the many cultures represented. The people remain the same, and their opinions remain the same, but they learn to get along with a larger mission in mind. Nothing is based on nationalities or gender. It's simply that you have your position, and the way you lean politically or religiously is a private matter, and there is no criterion no point of comparison here on board the ship. We don't deal very often with global issues. You need to keep this diversity. The moment you let one nationality become too big and too powerful, it usually causes distrust.

B1-C16-U2: United Nations: Peace and friendship. His advice to the United Nations is to end their folks to a place like this, where the task and team are important, and the young folks [working as staff on board] will return home better than before, be more tolerant, and be able to work in a more diverse and dynamic environment. There is more satisfaction here than working with self-defined standards. Each day offers different issues to deal with attentive service without being intrusive. He encourages the idea of the guests having the holiday of their life-time.

CHAPTER SEVENTEEN: Cruise Director Staff: *Work with, and become, a kid*

B1-C17-R4: Respect: Dinner bell? Working with different cultures gives you a new perspective on the world. You become more open-minded, see how people respond and suddenly realize people are so different, like a friend from Argentina, who eats dinner late. Her friend who lived in Britain most of her life typically ate dinner at 6:00 p.m. Now she eats dinner at 9:00 p.m.

CHAPTER EIGHTEEN: Beverage Department. *Sing, dance, serve*

B1-C18-G10: Guests: Guests are not strangers. Strangers? I don't consider guests to be strangers. They are long lost friends. They tell themselves, okay, we are going to meet some people. We are going to interact, to get to know them, know a little bit about their background, and I tell myself the same thing about them. That is why I am in this job. I am a people person. And it interests me when I can learn something about your culture, different things that you do in your country and how different it is in my country. With a huge smile and a little dance step to her walk, she says, Once you keep us happy, then we keep the guests happy. It works both ways!"

B1-C18-M10: Multi-cultural: Who makes whom happy? Of the roughly 2,200 crew members on board the Allure of the Seas, each member has an assignment geared to creating a happy experience for guests, and both the marine and hotel sides of the operation contribute to guest satisfaction. The fact that this company has blended crew from many countries only makes the accomplishment that much more amazing.

CHAPTER NINETEEN: Top management: *Who created this floating resort?*

B1-C19-L4: Leadership: Someone had to dream. We saw their fingerprints in the wonderful attitudes of the crew, and their commitment to excellence in serving guests. The leaders' blogs and industry reports about their philosophy underscore their strong principles about doing business. One could not interview a crew member of the cruise line without feeling the presence inside the room of the leaders who created the magic. Their mission of pleasing the guest in such a fashion that the guest will return embeds itself in each member of the team, from the veterans to the newest members.

CHAPTER TWENTY: Master: The official host: *You can be whatever you want in this world*

B1-C20-L5: Leadership: AIA confident captain. I don't leave them out there having to deal with the problems if we have a hurricane or storm. They are not the ones that should get those questions. I should be proactive and tell the guests why we have to skip the port or change the itinerary. So, yes, that's a little bit about management style. Top management sets the pattern, and like other key managers aboard, the captain feels he has the confidence and support of headquarters management, and they let him build and encourage his team with freedom to act, grow, and innovate. The person who has sailed with him knows from experience how steady and smooth the modern cruise vessel moves. The English poet, James Flecker, captured that feeling as he wrote, *"I have seen ships sail like swans asleep."*

CHAPTER TWENTY-ONE: Staff Captain: *Trust a huge team*

B1-C21-T4: Team/Family: *"Set your course by the stars, not by the lights of every passing ship."* Omar Bradley. I think it's very important for any type of rank, or any type of culture, to really respect and treat the others as a family.

B1-C21-F5: Friendliness: What about the bubble? People inside any "in group," like an ethnic or other group with similar kinds of people, feel like a bubble encloses them, and they may or may not look outside. Those who feel open to other cultures get outside that bubble, learn, and expand their knowledge. With respect to leadership training and styles, the "Building on Talent" program includes ways for managers to share information about their specialty with different people. He described the four pillars of financials, crew satisfaction, safety, and guest relations, and believes those who see the big picture will become more understanding of the various cultures and the way people develop in different ways.

CHAPTER TWENTY-TWO: Chief Engineer: *Keep the resort humming*

B1-C22-R5: Respect: Respect is in your power to give.

This engineer insists that his people respect and understand each person, regardless of their culture. The ship has its own culture, helping overcome the challenge of ethnic diversity. He took new crew on a tour and had some discussion going to a dining room a couple of days ago, and they were fascinated that they met someone from Indonesia; the next guy was from Trinidad and Tobago. Just in the engine room, we are probably about seven, eight different nationalities. So it goes, everywhere you walk on the ship; I would say you almost never meet two from the same country. With seventy-nine cultures represented, chances are slim."

B1-C22-A2: Age/Gender: Too old or young? Many cultures revere the elderly. This engineer's age could work against him elsewhere, but he has earned respect on merit, though younger than most Chief Engineers. He took over at age twenty-eight and supervised a mixture of crew ages. When I was first promoted, I was probably the youngest chief leader at the time. Ten years ago, when I took over as chief engineer and, you know, with my age then and the diversity of the crew on board, it could've been a challenge, but with the mix of crew that we had, it worked extremely well. It also comes down to who you are as a person.

B1-C22-A3: Age/Gender: Respect gender and age. Obviously, it comes through the way we put together training programs. It comes in the way we put activities on board, behind the scenes activities, crew activities, and the way we all respect each other. I think that's the key to the success. We make sure we respect each other.

B1-C22-A4: Age/Gender: A good time to be alive. His concern with possible age discrimination ties back perfectly to this book's reporting about cultural discrimination. The problems in areas involving age and gender are treated differently in many parts of the world. The solution he notes is the same as the ones the crew reports for language, cultural diversity, and ethnic discrimination: respect, lubricated by smiles and greetings.

B1-C22-T5: Team/Family: Friends pitch in. Each new crew member takes a two-week training course for "familiarization", but they supplement that formal training with supervisor counseling about life aboard ship, leading to a maturing experience. Mikael believes your responsibility extends to your own activities, on or off the ship at ports of call. The current fully trained crew might appear strong and self-confident but intimidating to a new person. He believes communication goes both ways, openly. If part of the crew looks overworked, others pitch in to help.

B1-C22-K2: Kindness: Kindness is natural here. He also gave the example of the third engineer, whose mom got sick, and the ship arranged for him to get home the next day. He and the crew will put all their strength into helping out. Management arranged all flight connections, and no one said that they would finish lunch first before making the arrangements. A trust exists that each team member will find help in time of need. Today, on this big ship, there exists a trained care team, whereas on smaller ships you would expect volunteers to help.

CHAPTER TWENTY-THREE: Marketing & Revenue Director: *Cash Flows*

B1-C23-L6: Leadership: A big responsibility. With respect to the hotel side, suppose someone asked you to operate, profitably, a floating hotel with 8,000 guests aboard. Perhaps the first task involves organizing hundreds of people into a skilled team. But a hotel, in this case, can't look like a static enclosure containing beds and bathrooms. It should please the guests and entice them to come back again soon. It should plan for different ages, genders, languages, and cultural tastes in food and entertainment. That plan needs to serve the basic creature comforts and needs for everything from health to clean clothes and linens. The plan needs sizzle. It needs to make the experience fun, educational, entertaining, and rewarding.

B1-C23-V2: Visiting: These contacts are precious. What does he do between contracts? Guests wonder about such things. Crewmates know much about their homelands and proudly share their knowledge while encouraging others to visit during time away from the ship. I went to ten countries in ten weeks and I never spent a day alone. I pulled into Romania and Bucharest. I've got my friend who's the restaurant manager picking me up from the airport. Another friend tells me, 'If you are in Romania, you call me. Within five minutes, I'll have an assistant waiter there to make sure you're okay.' He knows somebody in every city in Romania. So, anywhere I went in Romania, I knew I was okay, and then I cross the border and I make it to Bulgaria. I've got another friend, he picks me up puts me on a bus, sends me to meet up with another guy, the facilities manager on *our ship*. I meet him. He drives me back with his wife and his kid.

B1-C23-U3: United Nations: Why war? In this context, it seems unimportant that a person has a different religion from yours. The world's leaders might consider counting to ten, or even higher, before starting a war over religion or politics if their citizens could see and better understand the world by befriending someone from a different culture.

B1-C23-V3: Visiting: Bus travel. As a tourist, of course, you can take tours.

You will sleep where the guides designate and see the standard sights. However, suppose you took a bit of time with the waiter to ask about the country on his badge, and you learned enough to get interested. He or she might tell you about some fascinating places in their hometowns that the tourist doesn't normally see on the "one country each day" bus.

B1-C23-D3: Development: Career changes. The diversity thing doesn't stop at ethnicity. Cruise employees started their careers with occupations dramatically different from their current choice on the ship. "On one ship, a guy worked in the incinerator room, and he was a podiatrist back in Central America. He made more money working on the ship than being a doctor back home. There was a Somalian who had a PhD in Physics on ships in India. The guy was brilliant, and he's selling wine on the cruise ships in the dining room because it was a better opportunity for him."

B1-C23-G11: Guests: They meet crew daily. You have the chance to learn about their homes and cultures in Europe, Asia, South America, Africa, and the South Seas. They come to you, at your table and stateroom, and they will delight you if you take an interest in their lives and learn about the world, person by person.

B1-C23-K3: Kindness: Generous crew. Charities like Make-a-Wish Foundation benefit continuously with raffles (over $16,000 raised in June on one ship) and donation cards for guests and crew on all ships one month each year. This speaks volumes for their good citizenship from top to bottom. The crew alone contributed to "Make-a-Wish" the tidy sum of $3,652 in one week.

CHAPTER TWENTY-FOUR: Food & Beverage Manager: *We're upgrading our offerings*

B1-C24-M11 Multi-cultural: A big payroll. This manager came from Austria, but now lives in England. His career spans almost twenty years now, and he enjoys it, especially on this ship. He describes it as the biggest and the best, and his group represents the biggest division on board. His 1,073 people, working within food & beverage, contribute to the biggest percentage of the various nationalities. He remarked that some of the countries represented are at war with each other.

B1-C24-M12 Multi-cultural: A mix. The different religions, beliefs, and traditions, "just mold together". I think there's a mutual understanding to respect each other and to work together. It's also amazing for me to talk to my staff as well to find out about their backgrounds. We're like a family around here, and I don't mean in a cordial cheesy way. You know it's really true. Everybody understands what might be acceptable, what is common in one place, and what might be offensive to another nationality. You have crew members from completely different corners of the world who literally become best friends, develop a romantic relationship, and get married.

CHAPTER TWENTY-FIVE: Cruise Director: *It's all about having fun*

B1-C25-R6: Respect: Standards begin when hired. The cruise director, when asked about the diversified crew, says, "Maybe what the whole world needs is to go on a cruise to see how it's done. But it is true, I mean everyone is here to have a wonderful time, and our hiring partners, who have hired these great people around the globe, have talked to them about what we're expecting in regard to the cultural diversity and about how they need to make sure that they respect each other's traditions."

B1-C25-M13: Multi-cultural: Respect. He told us that Jamaicans always remind him that one word sums it all up. The word: "respect." His mission? People aboard should have fun, and the only true vote for that accomplishment occurs when they return. He loves the multi-national team he has working for and with him. Many of the performers have historically come from America, but he now lists many countries for his staff. He takes pride in the work Royal Caribbean International does for Haiti and several charities, and in the support given by the crew of each ship for these projects.

B1-C25-G12: Guests: Who comes first? He put a different twist on the sacred mission of pleasing guests. He said, "There is a great book out there I have never read, but the title, which I love, is, 'The Customer Comes Second,' because if your staff and crew are not happy, the customer will never be happy.

B1-C25-G13: Guests: Is it real? When are you going to quit and get a real job?
Are you kidding me? I say this is a real and s a dream job, because although it's hard work, everybody loves being here. You wake up every morning, you walk down the halls, whether it be with the guest or with the crew. It's a good feeling. So why would I want to go anywhere else? His mission involves persuading every guest to return to cruise again. And those return tickets represent the life blood of the business of cruising.

CHAPTER TWENTY-SIX: Housekeeping Manager: *On a large scale*

B1-C26-T6: Team/Family: Having fun. Crew are very proactive people. And they try to do a lot of crew activities, so, two weeks ago, we had people do their own thing. Some of the crew were playing music. Some of them were singing, dancing, doing ballet, or telling jokes. The management does a lot of stuff for the crew.

CHAPTER TWENTY-SEVEN: Concierge: *They just eat flowers*

B1-C27-W1: Workers: Three concierge workers serve the many suites. Creativity and imagination are needed, as a concierge simply fits the solution to the problem, and happy guests result. She says, my family is Italian, Spanish, Danish, and Portuguese, so all my great grandfathers came from different countries in the world and met in Brazil. We always joked that they met in a carnival. I don't think so. My family is very reserved.

B1-C27-O1: Opening up: Give friendship a chance. With respect to the interaction with crew, she says that everybody needs to be sociable after working so many hours a day. Sometimes, even though you're tired, you'll still go to the crew bar and sit by a table, and someone will come and talk to you. You will meet people that work with you along the way. So being a group on board is very important, if not the most important thing for you at sea. You are far away from your family and your friends. Even though internet is a great thing, it still doesn't get as close as you wish, to your family and friends. So, you bond with your shipmates, and this is for me one of the most wonderful things."

B1-C27-C3: Creativity: Be creative! She had an experience with a group of guests with special dietary needs that tested her creativity and knowledge of where to get help on board. When this group came on board, they already had everything prearranged. They had all restaurants booked and everything. They go to eat the first night of the cruise. The restaurant manager calls: do you have any information about one of these persons in the party of sixteen being vegan? These vegans only eat flowers; what am I going to serve them? This story has a happy ending with grateful guests, but, in between, getting the word out to food people all over the ship was a challenge!

CHAPTER TWENTY-EIGHT: Concierge: *A husband at work. We do everything for them*

B1-C28-F6: Friendliness: Getting to know you. Whatever they need, that's what we do. It doesn't matter what. That's the main part of the job. Obviously, we must socialize with them. They get to know us, and we get to know them also. So sometimes, we become friends. They even write us from home and let us know what their needs are.

CHAPTER TWENTY-NINE: Guest Services Officer: *A wife at work*

B1-C29-T7: Team/Family: Both act as a team. Though their languages differ (she speaks Bulgarian, and he speaks Spanish), they met on board and married. They have a common language of English and a common goal through their work. They deal with persons from many nations, and often she will refer a Spanish-speaking guest to her husband, while she gets his Russian-speaking referrals, plus some of those additional folks that speak the other five languages they have between them.

B1-C29-G14: Guests: Smile and take a breath. The cruise line treats fellow crew, as well as guests, as individuals, without regard to rank, cultural background, or whether a guest paid a thousand dollars or several times that much to board the ship. When a guest calls at 3:00 a.m. reporting a lost wallet, the crew helps, and the search begins at once. Each guest deserves that special feeling on departure that he or she had the best possible vacation.

B1-C29-G15: Guests: Different habits. Americans will share pictures of their families and other personal stories, whereas persons from some other countries may act more reserved. This gave clues as to how she and her husband, experienced guest-relations specialists, adjusted their communication to the cultures of the guests.

B1-C29-G16: Guests: A change in attitude. In their home countries, Turks and Bulgarians might act less friendly to strangers due to historical and political factors. Because working on a cruise ship requires staff get along with people of other nationalities, those who cannot adjust to employer policies may end up looking elsewhere for employment. Therefore, crew members of all nationalities must learn to treat their fellow workers and guests as individuals, not as representatives of "governments." The politics and religion back home cease to have relevancy to the task.

B1-C29-G17: Guests: A change for the better. Traditional prejudices and attitudes became a habit of the past, not useful in their current contacts back home.
A few years ago, an African had come to her home country for medical education, and locals saw the person as different, so the locals offered a cool welcome [unfriendly]. Now, she says, the colorful kids on the street seem to belong, despite the conservative nature of her people. So, it would seem that this world, with all its faults, might offer hope for tolerance and respect.

CHAPTER THIRTY: Beverage Department: *Be yourself*

B1-C30-T8: Team/Family: Attitude. When you're going to work on board, you have to be very tolerant with religion, politics, personalities, and cultures; otherwise it's not worth you moving from your country. It's been great for me. I have the ability of training my five languages every single day. It's been a great experience, the way people think, the way people act, the way people eat. If you do not have the tolerance to understand there are different cultures, you might as well just go home, because you're going to spend a hard time on board.

B1-C30-O2: Opening up: Here's a tip for meeting a Jamaican. After you greet one, he will just say, "Hey!" This seems natural for them, so let the conversation develop beyond this greeting and get to know them better. When asked about some universal way to get started with another culture, this waiter advised, "You have your personality; people understand your personality. If you understand other peoples' personality [accept people for who they are], it's easier for you to connect. So just be yourself."

B1-C30-F7: Friendliness: Smile. A smile always helps. When in the crew mess, he sits down and starts to talk to people he hasn't met yet, not just choosing people he knows. This helps him learn more every day about other people. We have people that have a lot of culture; they're well educated, but in their country, they cannot survive with all the qualifications they have. So, they have to come looking for a job, and they're willing to pick up the first shovel and dig the first hole. His advice proves the theme of this book. Start a conversation. Learn something.

CHAPTER THIRTY-ONE: Facilities Manager: *Fix it now!*

B1-C31-T9: Team/Family: Winners. When it comes to the cultures and diversities found onboard, the challenges test an individual's flexibility with people of many nationalities. Somehow, if you are black, if you are white, if I am small, or you are tall, we have come here to work and earn money, and at the end of the day, we are all winners if we work together.

B1-C31-L7: Leadership: Teach. I teach them all the tools they need. As a manager, also, it's important, not only that you're doing your job, but that you motivate your people. It's part of my job, and it's good to see people growing up and maturing in their work."

B1-C31-E9: English: The golden rule. Like many aboard, he speaks English as a second language. Guests might try to imagine reversing roles, trying to speak any language used by the cultures aboard ship. This could help them in cutting a bit of slack, if the wait staff or stateroom attendant stumbles over a word.

B1-C31-L8: Leadership: Fun. He shared his secret for motivating his team. First thing is, if fun is there, (it's always there), you have to work with them with fun, right? You have to acknowledge them, to acknowledge their good work. They make mistakes. Mistakes are always there. Nobody is perfect, so you have to teach them, and you have to give them the tools, not only the teaching. If one guy is hard headed, not willing to learn, we have these opportunity labs. It's like a bible from the company that helps the team.

B1-C31-L9: Leadership: Encourage leadership. The foregoing represents a textbook case of leadership, carrot-and-stick supervision, training, and attitude adjustment, delivered with humor and patience. Many guests wonder about the unique toilet design, and he explains about the vacuum system that uses less water, does the job, saves fuel and money, and repairs quickly. Sometimes during a week, the Facilities Management department has 200 issues with toilets, whether it involves guests throwing stuff in them, or failing to push the flush buttons hard enough.

B1-C31-E10 English: Similar backgrounds. I don't have any challenges when it comes to communication, or when it comes to cultures, but in my previous contracts, I worked with different nationalities where we had challenges when it came to their English speaking. So, what do we do with them? We put them in two-berth cabins with the good English-speaking crew. My crew has the same nationality.

B1-C31-U4: United Nations: Unfriendly countries? Two workers from politically unfriendly countries find it possible to cooperate in their job mission and leave the religious and political issues at home. Their home countries have no importance on board, a critical secret to success of the mission. Many readers will discover insights from this multi-cultural miracle of cooperation and respect, and they will observe and question situations in their daily life where they see a shortage of teamwork and friendliness.

CHAPTER THIRTY-TWO: Activities Manager: *Keeping fit and happy*

B1-C32-G18: Guests: What's new? A relaxing Activities 360 program has just rolled out twenty new activities after much research. They plan events for all ages and many nationalities and interests. The goal remains the same. The guest will have the best vacation ever. He commented that an empty ship, or one with a crew that does not smile, would not work, for the happy crew opens the door to happy guests.

B1-C32-G19: Guests: Relaxing. When you are on a cruise, part of the fun is meeting everybody from all over the world. It used to be just the crew, but now, on these ships, it is the guests as well. This ship is being advertised around the entire world.

B1-C32-F8: Friendliness: A universal greeting. He described the training for the "ten-foot rule." If anyone, guest or crew, comes within ten feet, you are expected to greet them with "Hi," and a smile, and this seems to make all the difference in the climate aboard the ship. Mitch described it this way, "I don't even know this guy, but I say "Hi" to him. He is from China or Russia, but it does not matter. We still say "Hi". And it just creates a bond that isn't really spoken of, but you're part of a team. This formula works!

B1-C32-M14: Multi-cultural: Lucky to learn this secret to life and success. For us to be living this experience working together, I would say I would never take this back or would never trade off anything with this experience, because I feel so cultured now with an understanding of all the different cultures in the world. And you can see where there's a difference in each culture. And you can see how people are brought up in different parts of the world just by working with them and knowing who they are.

B1-C32-G20: Guests: Change your life. Every one of those people will have a life-changing experience with people from every part of the world, as they pass by or talk and share things about their culture and traditions.

CHAPTER THIRTY-THREE: Musical Director: *No resort without music*

B1-C33-T10: Team/Family: A fascinating band. I feel like I've known them half my life already. He admired the talent of the sax player from Buenos Aires, Argentina and said, the drummer was from Canada. The piano player was from Bulgaria. It was the most diverse a group he had worked with.

CHAPTER THIRTY-FOUR: Casino Dealer: *What's your lucky number?*

B1-C34-C4: Creativity: Cut the deck. This talented guy knows the casino business, beginning in 1982. Part of a team of sixty-four casino workers from twenty-two nationalities, guests can call them "close," and no one will mind. There aren't a lot of crew members to go to dinner with you when you get off work at 3:00 a.m. Turns out, their "upside down" shifts force them to get to know each other. This is just a job, so we're comforting each other while we're away [at sea]. There is no nastiness or arguments. We just get along, and the management is fantastic as well. They cater to parties at night.

CHAPTER THIRTY-FIVE: Chef: *Delightful cuisine*

B1-C35-M15: Multi-cultural: Work hard and succeed. We point out the

humble beginnings, because this chef reported in modest fashion how he concentrated on becoming a high-quality crew member, learning everything well,
learning many new skills, passing numerous written tests, and rising to CDP1,
[chef with higher responsibility than CDP2]. He hopes to go even a step higher
on the world's largest cruise ship: a sous chef. He has sailed in Dubai and has
seen sights his family back home could scarcely imagine. With respect to the
diverse crew, he says, you get to know a little about their culture. It's really
good, because it shows you that no matter where you go, you have something
alike or in common in different areas. So, most of the time you are learning
what they really eat or what is their national dish. So, then, you're surprised
to know that what you have in your country, they have, because they ask you
about your Independence Day or what you guys do during the Christmas.

B1-C35-M17: Multi-cultural Eat and celebrate. Eventually, it's almost the
same thing most people do, the same thing. They get together, their family,
they eat and they celebrate." his team has folks from Indonesia, China, Africa,
India, Jamaica, Philippines, and Ukraine. He used to seek out Jamaicans, but
he now likes to mix with others. He referred to the training videos about China
and South America, and the way they help crew members to avoid offending
another culture.

B1-C35-M18: Multi-cultural: Careful with the humor! Whenever I joke, I always say certain things, and for them [foreigners other than Jamaicans] it is
no problem. When they [people other than Jamaicans] show you, you have to
say, okay, you cannot say that because they take it "serious". So, it's really
helpful. As time goes by, then once you start to rap with different nationalities, then you know exactly what they're all about, what they're like, and
what they don't like.

B1-C35-G21: Guests: A tasty option. When asked if a guest wanted to talk
to him about his culture and life, would he respond? Yes. Most of the time,
working in the Windjammer, your guest, you talk to them. They ask questions,
where are you from: Jamaica. What do you do? Sometimes we bring them during the tasting time [a time when guests are invited to the kitchen], to the
tasting table [samples of food for guests to experience]. They come and see
what we do before they eat. And they come to taste.

B1-C35-M19: Multi-cultural. Ask about languages. He says, Jamaica, it's
mixed. Our motto is out of many, one people. You have almost everything, different nationalities that build up Jamaica. French, Indian, Filipinos, Chinese,
it's all mixed. So, you come to Jamaica, you see a mixture of people. Even if
you don't take a kitchen tour, you most certainly will experience the results
of all this care and training when you lift your knife and fork aboard a cruise

ship. Compare the food and service to any five-star hotel. *Bon Appetit!*

B1-C35-G22: Guests: Guest or crew: celebrate diversity. Much can be learned from the inter-cultural success of cruise ship training and encouragement of respect between people from different backgrounds. The idea "we celebrate diversity," (repeated by the crew members in many ways), can seep into our lives, offering a ticket to new experiences with fascinating cultures around the world.

Conclusion

This is an unusual "business" book. While all managers and officers of an organization will most certainly want to know how the positive attitudes of people from the top to newly hired were encouraged, books 1 and 2 have universal appeal to any and all employees and even guests and family. Respect should not be locked in a safe. Unlike books with heavy texts suitable for an MBA student, this group of stories shows, one by one, how important each crew member could be to the success of the mission, which is to please guests and crew members alike, starting with a smile and a greeting. There are many other tasks delegated to crew members daily, and skills are required of each. But the attitude of warmth toward crew and guest is the foundation for each job well done.

These conversations with crew members tell us something about the environment created by the organization's leaders. They imply that people at the top of an organization have a clear vision of how to organize and motivate people, notwithstanding the language and customs differences of workers from many backgrounds and cultures. By seeking "how" the corporate culture can be spread and maintained, we might understand the recipe for the miracle of the "secret sauce" that the cruise line uses to encourage a blending of cultures and the creation of an unforgettable experience for the guests. There are people who spend much time interacting with guests and others whose main contacts are other crew members. The smile and the greeting symbolize the importance of every person aboard, and they open the door to further cooperation and friendship.

These stories reveal a crew culture that ensures "all hands work together" with cooperation and imagination, so guests have a happy and memorable cruise experience. On land or sea, the hospitality industry trains and motivates its people to please guests. This management team enjoys unusual success with cooperation among many different national cultures working on a single ship. Such a crew culture does not exist simply by accident or only because of good employee selection.

In dozens of stories, the answers to "how" vary with the individual, but the result is spectacular. New and veteran cruise guests can peek behind the scenes and learn about the ten-foot rule and many other secrets of the cruise industry. Supervisors and trainers can develop ways to encourage multi-cultural cooperation among their diverse employees. All types of entities, public, private and not for profit can learn from the ideas expressed by people who bear a striking resemblance to ourselves.

The author's interviewees reveal the secrets of how to motivate and train such employees. The United Nations, and the cultures they represent, could be another possible crucible for attempting to encourage respect for our differences. If our own organizations fostered the type of cultural admiration expressed on these pages, and our planet's nations applied the 10-foot-rule during all worldwide encounters, imagine the contagion that would foster! Perhaps this can be more than a business book if many readers took the stories to heart. It's amazing how a simple thing like employer standards for people earning a living could change the world's attitudes toward diversity. As one crewmember put it, "Somehow, if you are black, if you are white, if I am small, if you are tall, we have come here to work and earn money, and at the end of the day, we are all winners if we work together."

eBooks-keyed topics-Book2

Count	Book	Chap-ter	Topic	Name	A-Z	Chapters
2	B2	C08	A02	B2-C8-A2: Age/Gender	A	1-Master: Captain
3	B2	C51	B01	B2-C51-B1: Banking (Cash)	B	2-Staff Captain
16	B2	C51	C13	B2-C51-C13: Creativity	C	3-Chief Engineer
26	B2	C48	D10	B2-C48-D10: Development	D	4-Hotel Director
43	B2	C48	E17	B2-C48-E17: English	E	5-Safety
60	B2	C45	F17	B2-C45-F17: Friendliness	F	6-Maitre de Hotel
66	B2	C44	G06	B2-C44-G6: Guests	G	7-Doctor
71	B2	C49	H05	B2-C49-H5: Heart/Hugs/Habits	H	8-Financial Controller
77	B2	C41	i06	B2-C41-i6: Incentives	I	9-Cruise Director
85	B2	C42	J08	B2-C42-J8: Joy	J	10-Guest Services Manager
92	B2	C43	K07	B2-C43-K7: Kindness	K	11-Shoreside CPS Manager
101	B2	C41	L09	B2-C41-L9: Leadership	L	12-Deck Storekeeper
117	B2	C49	M16	B2-C49-M16: Multi-Cultural	M	13-Housekeeping Manager
129	B2	C30	N12	B2-C30-N12: Nationalities	N	14-Restaurant Manager
137	B2	C45	O08	B2-C45-O8: Opening up	O	15-Bar Manager
144	B2	C48	P07	B2-C48-P7: Promotion	P	16-Shore Excursion Manager
152	B2	C46	R08	B2-C46-R8: Respect	R	17-Hotel Cost Controller
155	B2	C50	S03	B2-C50-S3: Supervision	S	18-Duty Free Manager
166	B2	C50	T11	B2-C50-T11: Team/Family	T	19-IT Manager
167	B2	C34	U01	B2-C34-U1: United Nations	U	20-Dancer
171	B2	C32	V04	B2-C32-V4: Visiting	V	21-Band-Drums
178	B2	C41	W07	B2-C41-W7: Workers	W	22-Keyboard-Band
179	B2	C04	Y01	B2-C4-Y1: Youth	Y	23-Dancer

24-HK Jolly
25-Guest Services Host
26-Guest Services Host
27-Ordinary Seaman
28-Sanitation Officer
29-Chief Plumber
30-Engine Mechanic
31-Engine Secretary
32-ChefTournant
33-Asst Electrician
34-Asst Restaurant Manager
35-Asst Waiter
36-Galley Supervisor
38-Spa
39-Spa
40-Cabin Steward
41-HK Cleaner-Jolly
42-Light/Sound Technician
43-Head Pastry Chef
44-Bartender-Coffee Barista
45-Barwaiter
46-Home Office-Development
47-Crew Ambassador
48-Crew Ambassador
49-Chef
50-Head of Marketing
51-Hotel Director

Part 5: Extracts from Chapters in Book 2 [with topic names index]

INTRODUCTION

These are topical extracts from a book, "Crew Life", that shares a number of stories about fellow workers or crew members who live and work together aboard a floating resort. This extract is an aid to discussion leaders who are interested in topics that will help workers open up to people who are "different" and eventually befriend many of them. With some 51 people sharing stories about the job, family, and the experience of dealing with issues like languages, religion, customs, and social interaction, this series of extracts makes it easier to concentrate on several topics that may be a challenge to absorb from so many viewpoints. The topic labels are arbitrary and helpful only to a point. The goal is to absorb the stories and internalize the various feelings that make "different" become "exciting". Hopefully this analytical supplement to the story context will be helpful to HR in digging deeper into the various topics from many points of view.

If you are part of any type of team, whether for profit, government, academic or charity, the stories will likely help you and the team to perform better and perhaps help members to advance in their chosen occupation. The stories will certainly show what life is like aboard ship, and why it takes a month or so to get comfortable working at sea; but it will also satisfy a curiosity about the many skills needed to be a personal success in the hospitality or any other industry, while helping the employer succeed.

The setting is a medium size cruise ship. The people interviewed range from old timers to new hires, and they simply tell about their lives, jobs and family, [in book 2, but not necessarily in these extracts], but they all have in common the desire to get acquainted with their fellow crew members who just happen to be from over a couple dozen countries. That makes for some interesting friendships and reading.

The stories describe the process of befriending people who are different; by the last page, you will remember a number of examples showing how you, too, might be able to greet someone, perhaps born in a foreign country or culture, or at least "different" in some way. If you are curious about the cruise business, you have many more reasons to want to peek beneath the waterline of a cruise ship and learn about the lives of those in this industry who have the pleasant task of pleasing passengers aboard ship.

Curiously, the benefits are not limited to large companies. One sea-farer we know reported that his mom, a hairdresser, used the smile and greet friendliness and found her solo-worker business nearly dou-bled as a result. And this book reports many cases where promotions seemed to follow inclusion, teamwork, and leadership. Here Is the book's invitation to enjoy its adventure:

This ook, in traditional print and eBook versions, shares stories from crew and management on how to deal with life aoard, and how to apply the golden rule of respect for others who may have quite dif-ferent cultures from each other. The principles shared in this ook's crew comments are applicale to any group of people associated in any type of organization. They are intended to help the reader learn to ecome a etter repr   esentative for their employer and even their own families. Respect and smiles help the "smiler" as well as the "smilee"!

Chapters: 1-Master: Captain

2-Staff Captain

3-Chief Engineer

4-Hotel Director

5-Safety

6-Maitre de Hotel

7-Doctor

8-Financial Controller

9-Cruise Director

10-Guest Services Manager

11-Shoreside CPS Manager

12-Deck Storekeeper

13-Housekeeping Manager

14-Restaurant Manager

15-Bar Manager

16-Shore Excursion Manager

17-Hotel Cost Controller

18-Duty Free Manager

19-IT Manager

20-Dancer

21-Band-Drums

22-Keyboard-Band

23-Dancer

24-HK Jolly

25-Guest Services Host

26-Guest Services Host

27-Ordinary Seaman

28-Sanitation Officer

29-Chief Plumber

30-Engine Mechanic

31-Engine Secretary

32-ChefTournant

33-Asst Electrician

34-Asst Restaurant Manager

35-Asst Waiter

36-Galley Supervisor

38-Spa

39-Spa

40-Cabin Steward

41-HK Cleaner-Jolly

42-Light/Sound Technician

43-Head Pastry Chef

44-Bartender-Coffee Barista

45-Barwaiter

46-Home Office-Development

47-Crew Ambassador

48-Crew Ambassador

49-Chef

50-Head of Marketing

51-Hotel Director

eBooks: keyed topics-Book2

Count	Book	Chapter		Topic Name	[A-Z]
2	B2	C08	A02	B2-C8-A2: Age/Gender	A
3	B2	C51	B01	B2-C51-B1: Banking (Cash)	B
16	B2	C51	C13	B2-C51-C13: Creativity	C
26	B2	C48	D10	B2-C48-D10: Development	D
43	B2	C48	E17	B2-C48-E17: English	E
60	B2	C45	F17	B2-C45-F17: Friendliness	F
66	B2	C44	G06	B2-C44-G6: Guests	G
71	B2	C49	H05	B2-C49-H5: Heart/Hugs/Habits	H
77	B2	C41	i06	B2-C41-i6: Incentives	I
85	B2	C42	J08	B2-C42-J8: Joy	J
92	B2	C43	K07	B2-C43-K7: Kindness	K
101	B2	C41	L09	B2-C41-L9: Leadership	L
117	B2	C49	M16	B2-C49-M16: Multi-Cultural	M
129	B2	C30	N12	B2-C30-N12: Nationalities	N
137	B2	C45	O08	B2-C45-O8: Opening up	O
144	B2	C48	P07	B2-C48-P7: Promotion	P
152	B2	C46	R08	B2-C46-R8: Respect	R
155	B2	C50	S03	B2-C50-S3: Supervision	S
166	B2	C50	T11	B2-C50-T11: Team/Family	T
167	B2	C34	U01	B2-C34-U1: United Nations	U
171	B2	C32	V04	B2-C32-V4: Visiting	V
178	B2	C41	W07	B2-C41-W7: Workers	W
179	B2	C04	Y01	B2-C4-Y1: Youth	Y

Excerpts from: , 24-7" Multi-Cultural Workers Fin Diversity Recipe to Heal a Troule Worl :

CHAPTER ONE: Master: Captain: *I make sure the crew is well trained*

B2-C1-M01-Multicultural: Includes respect
"Do you talk to them about how they will be meeting people from many different cultures?"

We tell them that, especially for the crew, we are a multi-national, multi-cultural, and multi-religion environment. We have to work together in harmony and respect for each other. But I'm telling them, always respect. From the moment we respect others, they will respect us. This is a fundamental.

B2-C1-W01-Workers: Labor shortage helped by diversity. The ships are getting bigger, and they need more people. And to find people you have to employ from different countries and cultures. It's not really a problem so far.

B2=C1-F01-Friendliness: Personality traits.
"Do you have a magic formula as to how to get along with people?"

I think it's the personality of a person; that helps us get along with others. It's not really any formula. It's something that you do, naturally.

CHAPTER TWO: Staff Captain: *The deck hands appreciate me*

B2-C2-M02-Multicultural: How better? , Are there a vanta es in the cultural iversity¡ Woul it e etter if everyone were from the same culture¡ "
Oh, that is a lon   iscussion. It's always interestin , an   what   o you mean y etter¡ You mean more interestin   or safer or more eneficial in se   rvices to the   uest¡ What   o you mean¡

B2-C2-K01: Kin ness: First, learn to e patient and kind . I have learne how to e patient. To e even more patient than I use   to e, especially to e a mana er. The i   er the ship you have, the more   suor inates you have. An you are in comman . An   there are all the nationalities, lan ua es, an sometimes haits.

CHAPTER THREE: Chief Engineer: *We build a team, and it's like a family*

B2-C3-F02-Frien liness: New friends. Well, after so many years, there are no surprises. What is interestin   is that there are always new people in my life, an we uil   oo relations, make frien s, an   have happy memories. I love workin   with my team.

B2-C3-T01-Team/Family: Team is like family. I can trust my har -workin crew, an they trust me. We uil a team, an it's like a family, an for me, that is the most interestin part of our jo.

CHAPTER FOUR: Hotel Director: *I have smiles to give, which makes it a happy ship*

B2-C4-Y01: Youth: New, young workers; chance to mature and make friends. Yes, we have an impressive range of different cultures from around the world on board. From day one, new employees are eager to make new friends and learn the different languages, values and behaviors of their new colleagues and housemates/neighbors.

B2-C4-G01: Guests: Important and welcome. On board, we work like a family, and the guests are such an important part of our job, we want them to feel welcome to cruise again with us in the future.

B2-C4-C01: Creativity: Diverse set of solutions. Here at CMV we support the initiative and ambition of our team members, I believe it is important to nurture the creativity within a team as it will help to provide a more diverse set of solutions that can be adapted to deal with different specific situations.

B2-C4-H01: Heart/Hugs/Habits: Crew is heart of ship. You always need to be happy; the ship is made of steel and wood, but the heart of the ship is its crew.

CHAPTER FIVE: Safety Officer: *Charity begins with a tsunami*

B2-C5-E01: En lish: Different accents with English. I have a ifferent accent with the En lish lan ua e, ifferent from you in the Unite States. Different from my collea ues from Romania, ifferent from Chinese. Everyo y is suppose to know En lish, ut even that lan ua e ives us many pro-lems.

B2-C5-N01: Nationalities: Nationalities are transparent and get along. In cains, we'll have one cain with full crew insi e; one is In ian, one is Ukrainian, another one is a Romanian, an the fourth one is from In onesia. We try for the est, an they lea rn to et alon , on't they¡

B2-C5-R01: Respect: First respect me as a person. That is the main point that not only is for the oo ; I think it's also for our relationships. I hol to that octrine. I say to all the roups, on't respect me for my rank. First of all, you respect me as a person.

B2-C5-A01: Age: No age discrimination. When you are over a certain age, we throw you a different, let's say, part of the job. We need to do this from our human point of view.

B2-C5-K02: Kindness: Crew is generous and kind. I hear stories too when they have, for example, a tsunami in Asia; we collect money for them and for the families.

CHAPTER SIX: Maître de Hotel: *Have a vision for something next year and the next*

B2-C6-E02: English: Hard work but English is learned. We have to be good in English communication. These are the challenges that we always encounter, but for the work, it doesn't have any issue. Asian people and other cultures work hard, because they love the job. Some people, like a European, think that it's easy for them. I had never worked with Myanmar crew before, and once you see them improving and enhancing their skills, you know you have taught them the right way.

B2-C6-L01: Leadership: Lead so you can be replaced and move up. For my supervisors, I've always told them, share your knowledge. Don't be greedy. It's the same with the waiter. That person will replace you, and then you go up, and they will never forget, because you taught them the good ideas. So, they have a vision for something next year and the next year.

B2-C6-R02: Respect: Respect yourself first. Promoting is very important. In here, the crew are like my kids. Without them, I cannot survive, and without me, they don't know the next function. Sometimes there's a mistake, but we are not perfect. Everyone makes a mistake. If you care, you'll get them back. I'm not here to work only but to give them ideas. Before you respect the other person, you need to respect yourself first.

CHAPTER SEVEN: Doctor: *Our skills are a gift*

B2-C7-K03: Kindness: Advice to be kind and modest. But there's another advice which I will give. I want to give for other people, doctors, nurses, whatever. Just keep a low profile. Now, what do I mean y that; I mean, don't take it for granted that you are the best, because you have come up with experience, and just keep that low profile. Because I strongly believe that all of us, we are just tools in God's hands, and that it is just a gift, and you have to use it properly.

CHAPTER EIGHT: Financial Controller: *I help people from the heart*

B2-C8-J01: Joy: Joy to get to know others. When we have ifferent nation-alities for everyone, it wi ens your perspective. You et to know the culture of other people, their haits.

B2-C8-C02: Creativity: Pool your ideas from diversity. You know, like when you have a situation, how everyone rin s up their i eas. Because I also elieve in not just oin everythin on my own. It's very important to ele ate. That's how you have a epartment, an people rin in their i eas. You then choose etween which is the est, an which is the most efficient an easiest for everyo y. I elieve in iversity.

B2-C8-A02: Age/Gender: Female did not feel discrimination. , Have you seen any en er prolems in the cruise in ustryi"
Not really. I never face this prolem. In fact, I was always appreciate for my i eas or whatever I rou ht to the mana ement. This company has een fair for the past 11 years, an I woul n't e here if I i n't have these won er-ful osses in the hea office. The CEO was in hotel operations earlier. They have always een supportive. I really enjoy workin here.

B2-C8-S01: Supervision: See through their eyes and change yourself. So first you open your perspective to accept new i eas. Learn. We are learnin every ay until the ay we ie. No one is a superstar, an noo y's perfect. The minute you open up an chan e yourself, I'm sure everythin aroun you will chan e, ecause then you look at thin s in a ifferent way.

B2-C8-R03: Respect: Respect people, religions, everything. In In ia we have so many reli ions, an the people live in peace. We on't have a prolem with each other. It's only the overnments an the politicians who make these issues for their own veste interests. . . I et my oo thou hts from my elief. I am not ju in any other reli ion as I am very open.

B2-C8-R04: Respect: Words can be harmless. Respect yourself. They sai no one can harm you with their wor s. Only when you accept it an react o you harm yourself.

B2-C8-F03: Friendliness: Many friends are possible. An e frien ly with people; this is very important, ecause you can reak so many wron impres-sions y ein frien ly with someone. Sometimes your face may say some-thin , an when you actually speak to the person, you et to know the person etter. It's a ifferent impression. . . .Be open to all new thin s, e-cause it is the only way to row.

CHAPTER NINE: Cruise Director: *We try to make people laugh*

B2-C9-L02: Lea ership: A good leader helps people e comfortale, with a smile. You meet a lot of people every sin le ay. It's fascinatin to see where people are from. . . . Be firm, ut fair. I on't micromana e people too much. If I nee to e firm I will e. The uys support my team an create an atmosphere where people are happy. . . . My style is to try an make people lau h so I o silly jokes an make it as much fun as possile.

CHAPTER TEN: Guest Services Manager: *We don't say, 'No'*

B2-C10-G02: Guests: Keep them satisfied. Hospitality is the product that we offer. My focus is the customer services side. I'm dealing with everything that's going on.

B2-C10-M03: Multi-Cultural: Working together as equals. With respect to cultural diversity, there are different nationalities on board. We work very well together. We've got those from Eastern Europe, Asia, and all kinds of people from different countries. We all gel very well together, and I think everybody has the same attitude and the same mentality, and that we're here to serve the guests. We're here to do a job. . . . And then we all look at each other as equals as well. . . . I treat everybody as I would want to be treated.

B2-C10-W02: Workers: Quality treatment attracts workers when they are scarce. We've got so many nationalities. We're having a lot of people now coming from other cruise lines that have had crews for quite a few years. We are attracting workers, and they're coming over.

B2-C10-i01: Incentives: Not all incentives are monetary. There are things in place to give motivation. It's helpful to actually be praising them. I think sometimes that gets forgotten as well. We tend to do more now in praising our crew. Well done. Good job.

B2-C10-P01: Promotions: Start from the bottom so when promoted, you know how to train. Then, with the restaurants, you'd be joining as junior waiter and then to senior. There is promotion from within. I think it's good to promote from within, because they know the product more. The people they might be supervising know that they're there; they've worked for this company, and now they've moved up.

CHAPTER ELEVEN: Shoreside CPS Manager: *I get them on board*

B2-C11-W03: Workers: Treat the workers as a most valued asset. It is important for the new crew to know there is someone who will look after them oth efore an after oar in the sh   ip. . . . They will or anize foo an rinks for crew. Some of the crew have never een outsi e their own country efore.   . . . The crew is like family, as they move from ship to ship workin .

<u>CHAPTER TWELVE: Deck Storekeeper: *I Follow the R.I.T.E. Way*</u>

B2-C12-T02: Team/Family: Close association with fellow crew memers. For four years now, Fa li says, the ship ecame my secon family.

B2-C12-J02: Joy/Cultures: Curiosity. Fascinating traditions. , You like learnin aout all the tra itions of the many nat ionalities on oar ¡ " Like in Bali, they have the kecak ance, so we like sharin that ance, maye in the crew talent show. The Day of Silence, a ck in Bali, is calle Nyepi which is a Hin u celeration. For 24 hours the people oserve total silence. The streets, an even the airport, are close . The women cook for ays in preparation of not havin any li hts on, usin the stoves for cookin , or makin noise. The ni ht efore is the o oh -o oh para e whose purpose is to purify the natural environment of any spiritual pollutants.

<u>CHAPTER THIRTEEN: Housekeeping Manager: *Enjoy the Free Time.*</u>

B2-C13-W04: Workers: Happy workers are the est recruiters . In 2013, I talke to a frien ; we rew up to ether. He was workin with the CMV, an I aske him if he can put me in contact with the a ency. ¥Employee recruitin ı[I starte a ain in 2013 when I joine the ship as a cain stewar . Step y step, year y ye ar, I went up on the la   er.

<u>CHAPTER FOURTEEN: Restaurant Manager: Welcome to my family</u>

B2-C14-L03: Lea ership: Leadership is the total package. He seems to e everywhere with his smile an an eye for supervision. His messa e for new people is: , Welcome to my family. I am not only a restaurant oss; I am as well a person who listens to prolems an tries to solve them an help. You will learn all you nee to know step y step. Mistakes are no prolem if you take them to learn."

<u>CHAPTER FIFTEEN: Bar Manager: *If you give, it all takes place naturally*</u>

B2-C15-P02: Promotions: An expanding employer offers opportunities. My evaluation move me up one more step to arten er. For two years in a row I worke as arten er an then move up to assistant ar mana er, then ar mana er. I move very fast up the la   er. I'm quite lucky.

B2-C15-F04: Friendliness: Project friendliness into everything. I elieve that hospitality is somethin that only you, as a frien ly person, can o. I e- lieve that if you on't like what you are oin , you ha etter fin somethin else.

B2-C15-W05: Workers: Attitude predicts success. We nee to have that pleasure to say, yes, I'm oin to work. It's attitu e for those thin s, isn't it¡ Goo attitu e. If you ive, it all takes place naturally.

B2-C15-i02: Incentives: Pay, vacation at work, and seeing the world are rewards for a job well done. If they want to uil a future an e as stron as possile, they nee to un erstan that everythin that they're oin , it's for themselves. I call workin on the ship a pai vacation, ecause you're pai for what you are oin onoar . Then in the same time you have the oppor- tunity of seein the worl .

B2-C15-i03: Incentives: Compliments add value to compensation. I feel like when you see the uests enjoyin themselves, it's a oo feelin when you et oo comments re ar in your crew memer s. It makes you feel prou that you are oin your jo.

CHAPTER SIXTEEN: Shore Excursion Manager: *It's boring without challenges*

B2-C16-M04: Multi-Cultural: Both crew and guest are from many cul- tures. The excursion clients come from ifferent cultures an are ifferent types of people as well. They have ifferent min sets an mentalities. . . . It epen s on the weather an thin s, ut enerally it is a oo customer relationship with the passen ers we have.

B2-C16-J03: Joy: You can feel the excitement. When you o to the coun- try, an see how it is, feel the atmosphere an talk to the local people, that is ifferent from what you rea from the ooks. You et a new insi ht an etter un erstan in , which is a way to wi en your own knowle   e experience. I think travelin , especially on the worl cruises, chan es the mentality of people.

B2-C16-F05: Frien liness: It's a chance to meet new friends. We have many ifferent nationalities in the crew, an sometimes you have many people from your own country, ut often you on't. It makes you like a family. You talk to them, eat with them, spen a lot of time with them.

B2-C16-N02: Nationalities: You meet other nationalities without a costly itinerary. Now I know many people from there. They tell aout the culture of their countries. You et to know how they are as well. You will see some typical features aout this nationality or another nationality. I think it's very enrichin .

B2-C16-J04: Joy: You can find many friends. I'm happy with my relationships. I'm enerally without much to complain aout; the jo can e stressful sometimes, ut it's a part of it. Any jo woul e stressful, an sometimes you have to o thin s which you are not fon aout or on't want to o. I th ink it's orin without challen es.

B2-C16-J05: Joy: Meet new friends in China. All people are ifferent, ut at the same time, human nature is similar isn't it¡ It's interestin to have ifferent connections an to learn ifferent cultures an to have frien s in ifferent parts of the worl . But I think at the same time, you nee to make an effort for this as well. You nee to compromise, an many thin s require us to e open min e , ecause what is acceptale in some countries may e unacceptale in othe rs.

B2-C16-R05: Respect: You can respect their rules. Accept them, rather than rin in your own worl to them while tryin to promote it. That takes an effort as well. . . . You're very much in control of your thou hts an lo ic. The worl appreciates that.

CHAPTER SEVENTEEN: Hotel Cost Controller: *Predicting a need for eggs*

B2-C17-G03: Guests: Know your customer when ordering food. , How o you know in the first place how to uy for a Worl Cruise¡ " Experience counts a lot. Sometimes we have to uess. For example, in Europe, sometimes we have more Scottish or Irish. We have to know what kin of eer the Irish like. . . ., What aout foo . Different cultures like to eat ifferent kin s of foo ¡ " Meat is meat ut fixe in ifferent styles, with a va riety of spices.

CHAPTER EIGHTEEN: Duty-Free Manager: *Every day we learn something*

B2-C18-H02: Heart/Hu s/Haits: Haits and customs are fascinating. We are from all over the worl , an every country has its own haits. An estures. I use to work with Italians. They use more of the han s. Some of the crew are more hu in . Some people on't have this in their culture. Some cultures on't want you to stan too close. Latino people are very frien ly, very warm. They are touchin an hu in . Nor ics are not that way, ut that oesn't mean that they're not frien ly. They're not use to ein so warm. I worke with

Polish people, an they were very cool. But, when you talk, you realize that actually they are not.

B2-C18-O01: Openin up: Breaking the ice. , How o you reak the ice an start talkin with someone¡ " I know it comes naturally. I on't know. I will just o. I on't think that I will istur the m. I think when we start to have a conversation, it will e natural; I on't just o an ask or say hello. There comes a moment when you may sit at the same place, an you start to talk.

CHAPTER NINETEEN: IT Manager: *Use the resource carefully*

B2-C19-K04: Kindness: A welcome on the gangway. I meet with them and say, first before you buy internet, come talk with me about the best ways to use the Wi-Fi. One thing I've learned is that I feel very needed here. This is one of the most essential services the ship offers.

CHAPTER TWENTY: Dancer: *We are all in the same boat*

B2-C20-N03: Nationalities: Big world; sometimes lonely. I am the only En lish ancer, so all the rest are Ukrainian or from Belarus, so they all speak Russian. . . . We all have to help each other, ecause we are all in the same oat ¥[an everyone ets a little it homesick sometimes an are worrie that they can't o somethin . . . . I never met people from so many nationalities, so you just on't really think aout it. I t's opene my eyes to lots of new cultures. Everyone ets on so well. We're all so ifferent, an there are never any prolems. Most people speak a oo level of En lish, s o we can all communicate well.

B2-C20-D01: Development: You can grow from the challenges. From four years a o, I"ve efinitely ecome more confi ent as a person, ecause you have to talk to passen ers all the time. Proaly, if you aske me to o this on my first contracts, I ha to e a it nervous.

B2-C20-O002: Opening up: You can initiate contact. For new crewmemers, I" say just e nice to everyo y. I just smile an say hello to everyo y, e-cause when you first o on, you on't know who anyone is. . . . , What are if-ferent customs of the Ukrainians that you are not use to¡ " They like to keep to themselves an uil a arrier, ut once you reak own that arrier, they are amazin .

CHAPTER TWENTY-ONE: Band-Drums: *It's nice to have some fresh challenges*

B2-C21-E03: English: No common language. Then what? , Which of the cultures or nationalities o you seem to et alon with¡ " I like the Ukrainians with the an , an there"s one uy in the an from the Philippines. The lan- ua e arrier is really iffic ult. We somehow mana e, an it all comes to- ether an soun s incre ile. When you reak it own, the uitarist an myself can"t communicate in lan ua es. I can"t speak Russian, an he can"t speak much En lish. We can just sit own, put out the music that I woul play, an it soun s amazin .

B2-C21-H03: Heart/Hugs/Habits: You adjust to habits of cultures. You see all these ifferent cultures, an it is amazin . Everyone just works for one i team. I just smile to them, an they"ll smile ack, an everyon e"s a i fam- ily. Everyone ets on really well. , Are there customs of other cultures that you fin   ifficult to eal with, or really interestin ¡ " With the an , they are kin of strict, like everythin is lack an white. I coul have a eate with someone for an hour, an they woul just say no, it's this way or that. It's not a a thin , just interestin .

CHAPTER TWENTY-TWO: Keyboard-Band: *Music Is the Best Language*

B2-C22-N04: Nationalities: You can do it! My position is show-an mu- sician, an every ay I have a rehearsal. It is not easy, ecause of the iffer- ent nationalities an lan ua es. But we like what we o, an it is a oo experience to o somethin to ether.

B2-C22-J06: Joy: You can learn of customs. , Do you ever talk aout cus- toms at Christmas or New Years¡ " Yes, of course. We talk aout how we cele- rate. It's very interestin to learn aout another country.   . . . Now I have a lot of frien s across the loe. It"s my secon contract, an I have a few frien s from my first contract year. . . . , Woul you like to visit your frien 's country as well¡ " Yes. Everyo y says come to my country. Especially in Ukraine, it's very easy.

B2-C22-E04: English: You can overcome English deficiencies and help oth- ers to learn. , Do you like all the variety of cultures on oar , since it's so har to communicate with people¡ " It"s ecause I think everyo y has a lot of time for un erstan in .

CHAPTER TWENTY-THREE: Dancer: *Dancing that comes from the soul*

B2-C23-J07: Joy: Rehearsals; then come see the world. , Why i you choose a sea jo instea of workin on lan ¡ " Because I like travel an the ship was a natural place.

CHAPTER TWENTY-FOUR: Housekeeping Jolly: *My job is to make everyone happy*

B2-C24-N05: Nationalities: Many nationalities offer the chance to learn. , There are over 20 ifferent crew nationalities. How o you communicate with them¡" We on't have many prolems to communicate with the other crew or the passen ers. The crew, for instance, learns that we have ifferent nationalities on oar , an we nee to know their communication. Like certain thin s mean somethin in their lan ua e, an what is frien ly in their lan ua e mi ht e unfair in another one. So, we are tau ht to e frien ly; only expect the normal thin , an it ecomes a hait; wh en you et to know the person for one week &the har est time(, then over a perio of time they ecome like rothers or sisters. We all must know each other.

B2-C24-N06: Nationalities: Learning is fun. It"s really nice to learn aout ifferent cultures an ifferent countries. You et to see really ifferent places. Like I have seen most parts of the worl in my five years of contracts. Even when I am home, I take the ike an o in In ia.

B2-C24-K05: Kindness: Pass it on. I always ma e sure that I am there to help that person even if they are a ifferent nationality, so that he oesn't feel what I felt when I first joine .

B2-C24-M05: Multi-Cultural: Like a University for growth. I o like this situation of many cultures, ecause you et to learn aout ifferent thin s. So, when the opportunity came to min , I took it, an I i want to learn aout ifferent people, ifferent cultures, an ifferent places, an I ot to see that personally. , So, curiosity is a oo thin to have for the people comin a oar ¡" Yes, you et to learn aout lan ua es, others' ehavior, the way they talk; an anyone who tells you there is no pastime on the ship, they are so wron . There are so many thin s to learn.

CHAPTER TWENTY-FIVE: Guest Services Host: *You learn about their home*

B2-C25-F06: Friendliness: Friendships are easy to make in the workplace. When you come on oar you meet loa s of people. I think you have to e a social person to work on a ship. You on't know anyo y, an you must fin it easy to talk with people. Everyone here is so frien ly an totally ifferent than workin on lan . I on't know why, ecause many are in little roups of their nationalities. But they accept you. I have frien s from other countries.

B2-C25-V01: Visiting: You can personally visit countries and learn. I"ve never foun anyone I haven"t ot alon with. . . . You can see them on the internet or in a ook, ut to actually o there an see them in real life is totally ifferent. I quite like the Asian cultures after seein their temples an learn-in aout their history.

CHAPTER TWENTY-SIX: Guest Services Host: *If happy, they come back*

B2-C26-N07: Nationalities: Much in common with all. When you are here on oar , you make so many frien s that have common interests with you, even thou h they are from Ukraine or Romania.

B2-C26-N08: Nationalities: Growth happens. You et a lot of insi ht into lives from other cultures. The more you know, the more you can un erstan an can relate to them. I think that just makes you row as a human ein .

B2-C26-M06: Multi-Cultural: Weddings? , Do you ever talk aout customs an holi ays with crewị " I talke with the Hotel Director. He is from In ia an tol me that at a normal we in , you woul invite literally thousan s of people. He ha a very small we in an invite 1500 people.

B2-C26-N09: Nationalities: Hungry for adventure? Last ni ht, we ha Ukrainian ni ht; we have Latino ni ht an In ian ni hts. Then they feature some of the foo s from those countries. They chan e their foo s. They may chan e the music an ecorations.

B2-C26-F07: Friendliness: Being a real friend. We always try to help each other out, support each other.

CHAPTER TWENTY-SEVEN: Ordinary Seaman: *You have to respect each other.*

B2-C27-R06: Respect: Respect fits all situations. This is a new an iffer-ent experience for me. On ships like this, we on't have nationalities. We are all or inary seaman with the same lan ua e, an everyo y is the same. It is our main rule. You have to respect each other.

CHAPTER TWENTY-EIGHT: Sanitation Officer: *Training starts with safety first*

B2-C28-N10: Nationalities: Flexile acceptance of differences. There are five nationalities workin in this epartment. They are from Ukraine, In ia, Seria, In onesia, Burma; sometimes Filipinos come to help. It's a ifferent ack roun , ifferent attitu e, ifferent ehavior, ifferent kin s of styles an cultures. Everythin is ifferent.

B2-C28-N11: Nationalities: Why are we here? So, in this trainin , we are always tellin the people, the crew, how to ehave, an we make them un erstan we are all comin from a ifferent nationality, ut why are we here all to ether¡

B2-C28-G04: Guests: Because of the guests. This is the point. We know how to make sure the uests are happy. Why we are here is eca use of the uests. The uest is the one payin everyo y's salaries. If we on't have the uest, no jos.

B2-C28-T03: Team/Family: Flexile; after one -month, they team up and can overcome the little difficulties they face. Then, ecause they're work-in with the ifferent nationalities, they iscuss their prolems, an they share the cain.

CHAPTER TWENTY-NINE: Chief Plumber: *You can use ideas from other cultures.*

B2-C29-O03: Opening up: Be open to ideas. , Is it har for you to work with the ifferent cultures¡ " No, not in my experience. It's not har . It's oo also to work with the ifferent cultures, to learn the cultures that sometimes you can a opt; you can use their i ea in your country as well. Once I worke with someone in Flori a; now he's in my epartment. Also, I work with Ukraine, Greece, an In onesia people.

B2-C29-T04: Team/Family: Accept and include Yes. I have some In onesi-ans on the team. You have to work like rothers. We on't have a choice who we work with, so we have to e professio nal.

CHAPTER THIRTY: Engine Mechanic: *I have a chance to learn*

B2-C30-N12: Nationalities: Understand the job. , An what aout workin with the people from ifferent cultures an nationalities¡ Is that any kin of a prolem¡ " Never, ecause we un erstan the jo. You have a oo thin , an to ether we et it correct.

B2-C30-V02: Visiting: Flexible , Do you ever et off the ship an visit these ifferent countries an cities like in Japan¡ " Yes, we have a chance to o an to walk aroun , an it's interestin . , If you ha a chance, an it cost you no money, what country woul you like to o to¡ " Cana a. It's a oo place.

CHAPTER THIRTY-ONE: Engine Secretary: *Love first your job*

B2-C31-V03: Visiting: I'd like to go there. , Is it har to eal with the if-ferent cultures¡ " No, I love it. I am happy to know the other nationalities. I have a nice In onesian frien . I aske what is their culture so I have some knowle e, ecause maye some ay we'll o there, or to Ukraine, to In   one-sia. I have respect, an this is numer one for me. No matter what is your na-tionality, it is your culture: if you have respect, it's not a i prolem. When I was rowin up, I met people from many nationalities, so I was alrea y fa-miliar with many ifferent cultures.

B2-C31-F08: Friendliness: Help them feel comfortable and included. , When you have a new crew memer comin into your area, o you try an o somethin to help them feel comfortale¡ " I like to say the Philippines is numer one in hospitality. We will ask someone what they nee , an if they nee some help, we et them comfortale an not to e afrai with us. Okay. Just come with us. Ask me what you nee .

B2-C31-O04: Opening Up: Greetings open the door. I feel that everyo y is my frien . Because of this, I feel I am approachale. If I pass in the morn-in , I say oo mornin , how are you¡ Startin there, you can e a frien . Everyo y who nee s help, I try to help, an this is a i accomplishment for me.

CHAPTER THIRTY-TWO: ChefTournant: *Learn each culture's food*

B2-C32-E05: English: Food is a gateway to communication. I like this. You speak in this lan ua e, an when you have ifferent ones, then you can learn. It's a it of this lan ua e an that lan ua e. Different lan ua es are interestin ., Then o you have to learn each culture's foo ¡ " Yes. When I was a little it alone at home, I ot rea y for the German an other uests, an then I trie out menus for In ia.

B2-C32-V04: Visiting: Visits help seal friendships and understanding. , Durin your three months off, o you ever et to ether with people that have een on the ship that you know, so you actually o where they are or maye they want to come an visit you¡ Has that happene ¡ " Yes. I invite an assistant for one month at home.

CHAPTER THIRTY-THREE: Assistant Electrician: *It's like a team*

B2-C33-W06: Workers: Happy workers recruit friends & family. "Is there somebody on the ship that is your role model; someone that you look up to?" Well just my cousin. I have family on this ship, because my cousin, he is an electrician. My father was also a Chief Electrician on cruise ships, and it's something that my family background comes from: a captain and two fellow electricians.

B2-C33-T05: Team/Family: Professionals cooperate. I have to do my job. The other person has to do their job as well. If you're done, you communicate with each other. If there is no teamwork, nothing is going to come out.

B2-C33-M07: Multi-Cultural: Color and religion are not relevant. It's a family. You have got to work as a team. On this ship, you don't put in front of a person their nationality, their religion, or the color of their skin. From my part I don't put any of that in front of anyone.

B2-C33-D02: Development: Maturity includes overcoming differences. I don't care if you are Jewish or a Muslim. If you cannot see it that way it's unfortunate, because this is where you live. This person is here for the same reason you are. You either stick together or go home. You have to work with the other person. Because also the job has to get done, and they can help you to do your job. The company hired you to do a job. They didn't hire you to judge people for who they are or why they are. You respect people for what they are.

B2-C33-i04: Incentives: The most powerful incentives aren't money. There is some satisfaction that someone is thankful for some little thing you did for them.

CHAPTER THIRTY-FOUR: Assistant Restaurant Manager: *Better than the UN*

B2-C34-U01: United Nations: Start at local levels for peace. The fun part is working along with these people with different nationalities. I can see that we do better than the UN as far as culture diversification. Like, for example on other ships, we had a mixed crowd, and that included a lot of kids. On others, we served luxury. We now cater to different clients. But that, along with the crew, is action packed.

B2-C34-F09: Friendliness: The secret is support. Whenever a new arrival comes, we are told to support him; he is new. The word new, that means we start from scratch. We take them everywhere. There's an orientation. When the new person comes in as an assistant waiter or a buffet attendant, we don't put them on the floor straight. We give him some back-of-the-house jobs, so he can gain the confidence to make friends and to talk.

B2-C34-L04: Leadership: Both the buddy and newbie learn leadership. We have this buddy system. If any problem happens, you can go to him. He's your buddy. He will be helping you. He'll be guiding. He reports to us that certain questions were asked, and these are the answers given to him. He comes to know how his performance is doing. The feedback is given to the crew member.

B2-C34-i05: Incentives: Personal satisfaction: Nobody comes here without getting rewards. It can be monetary or satisfaction. At the moment, for me it's satisfaction, but they see my job, and I don't have to project more.

CHAPTER THIRTY-FIVE: Assistant Waiter: *Honor a passenger's request*

B2-C35-P03: Promotion: A strong incentive to support the team mission. I would like a promotion in my next contract. This is my second contract. My last contract I worked as a buffet attendant in the bistro.

B2-C35-F10: Friendliness: The culture makes smiling easy. "So how do you keep a positive attitude when you are working with strangers?" Because it's my culture. My parents teach how to get along with many people. Everything is okay. We are always smiling.

B2-C35-E06: English: Differences and language hurdles. "Do you find it hard to deal with passengers who have different customs and traits and speak differently?" No, but sometimes, I just can't understand, and I go slow.

B2-C35-M08: Multi-Cultural: Food leads to conversation and respect. U "Have you made friendships outside of the Filipino group and tried their foods?" Yes, I have. Some from Burma and Indonesia. Most of the time I try Indian foods. Special curry. Especially spicy garlic. I like it, because my friend, before I came back here (on my second contract), is an Indian guy.

CHAPTER THIRTY-SIX: Galley Steward: *I just like people*

B2-C36-E07: English: To manage is hard. Need English skills practice. "Do you find it hard, working with people from different cultures?" Yes, because some of the guys, they have some problems, like language problems. They don't understand. We just try to speak with them. We find it's a little bit harder, but we can manage it.

B2-C36-M09: Multi-Cultural: Gestures can be hurdles. , And did they have gestures that they use? Hand motions and some customs that are hard to deal with as well?" Sometimes it's very hard to explain to them. Because, in different cultures, we have some different signs. But they understand. Everybody understands. When we try to speak with them most properly in English, they can learn some things. When they came here, they didn't know much about English.

B2-C36-F11: Friendliness: Talking is the lubricant for respect. My friends come to my cabin, and we talk, and that makes me happy. I can like everybody. I like to make friends from other countries as well. . . . I just like people and to make new friendships.

B2-C36-E08: English: Language opens doors to "mixing". I don't know about the other people's ideas, but some of the people don't like to mix with other people. I cannot really say that about the people I can mix with. The guys are not going to exist with them unless they have the language. It's not easy to understand them. The language is a big issue. It's interesting.

CHAPTER THIRTY-SEVEN: Assistant Galley Steward: *I practice English*

B2-C37-E09: English: English requires time and tutoring. , Was it har for you to et use to workin with ifferent cultures¡ " Yes, ecause on the eck oat I ha more free om. Here we have to think more aout our work, an we are takin care of people. I i n't speak any En lish when I starte . Now that this is the secon contract, I can speak a little it more En lish. At first when my officer tol me to o somethin , I i n't know what he was sayin .

B2-C37-E10: English: Use it or lose it & read eBooks. I learn from watchin movies an rea in ooks. My teacher fr om ack home writes me every ay an tells me to practice an rea . My cain mates are oth from Myanmar, an we practice speakin En lish a lot. We share wor s we've hear urin the ay that we on't un erstan an help each other.

CHAPTER THIRTY-EIGHT: Spa: *They give us a chance to travel*

B2-C38-E11: English: Amazing blend of words! The English on board the ship is not really clear English; we call it ship language. We are using words from everywhere like Poland, Ukraine, India and Indonesia. You can go to another ship, and the crew knows the same language. I couldn't believe I was in the Caribbean Sea; later I was in Europe. My friends from school went to Australia. There's a lot of different cultures.

B2-C38-C03: Creativity: One culture. One solution. "Do you like the idea of working with many different cultures, or would you prefer that everybody was Polish?" I know from times when I've been in Poland. I thought it's only one way of thinking, and I was thinking the same as every single one from my country; later on, I realized it's not healthy.

B2-C38-L05: Leadership: Question the rules. There were a lot of rules. Now I'm coming back home, and I'm saying, no, don't think like that. It's not working, so go out from the rule. The ship, it's teaching how to treat people, how to understand people more. It's a good school for life. Maybe my son I will send, or my daughter. I don't know, because I don't have children yet.

B2-C38-L06: Leadership: What about rules that consider the world? Then everybody is in the "in-group". I think it's easier to live with people when you know that your rules are, not from your home, but rules for all the world. You learn to treat people better, and you are not judged.

B2-C38-F12: Friendliness: When communicating, you are helping. "Communication helps a relationship, because the people are really trying. There is an implication that you are going to help?"

<u>CHAPTER THIRTY-NINE: Spa: *I know how to adapt in a difficult situation*</u>

B2-C39-M10: Multi-Cultural: How to treat people. , Do you think there are a vanta es in all the ifferent cultures in the cultural iversity ein on oar ¡" I efinitely think so. I think if y ou row up, you shoul not have only one set of i eas of, say the perspectives aout what's ri ht or what's wron ; or what wor s are hauntin , especially how to treat people.

B2-C39-L07: Lea ership: Leadership includes changing yourself to adapt to reality. If I think aout it, it opens your min to see how other people o thin s, an what's etter or what's worse. For example, in this spa, espe-cially, we have a lot of Serians now, an it's een very interestin to see. I knew them as personal in ivi uals efore this cruise, an now they roup to- ether. So as personal in ivi uals, I've sometimes thou ht they were very i-rect people. I realize that it's actually just a part of their culture, so it chan es my min to maye not always e so sensitive, or not to feel offen e or what-ever. Now I coul just take it as it comes, an it really chan e my way of un- erstan in how you can take thin s; you have to rea people in a ifferent way.

B2-C39-C04: Creativity: Creative solutions include relationships. Because you are in pulic service, a perspective is very important for you as a person, ecause you're not alwa ys oin to e in a place that's easy, or you are eal- in with people only when you feel like it.

B2-C39-F13: Frien liness: Flexil e passengers. So even if you're tryin to put up a face, an you look happy, people respon very well to that, an then you can also take that experience an roa en it.
B2-C39-K06: Kin ness: Unexpected warmth. Sometimes you cannot o to lunch, ecause you're workin too much or whatever. Someone will rin you

a san wich; it's very nice. People make a point to reet you or say Bon Appetit.

B2-C39-M11: Multi-Cultural: It's OK initially to e with "folks like you ".
, Suppose you ha a chance to talk to someo y who just came aoar in
any capacity. What kin of a vice woul you ive them aout multicultural situations¡ How to act¡ " It woul   epen where the person comes
from. If it's someone who actually is from a nationality that's alrea y on
oar , I woul think they woul n't have too many prolems slottin into a
 roup that alrea y speaks their lan ua e, or knows their culture.

B2-C39-E12: En lish: Practice. Practice. The only way to improve in
En lish is to use it. An for some people it epen s on why they are here;
maye to travel or improve their positions.

B2-C39-F14: Frien liness: Hiring folks who can smile is OK. A person
who ot me on the ship tol me to come on the ship, ecause he sai you
have the ri ht personality for the ship. I think I'm a very open-min e
person. I'm a very frien ly person. I know how to a apt in a ifficult situation. That makes a ifference. Plus, I love to travel, an any cons are outwei he y the pros.

CHAPTER FORTY: Cabin Steward: *The culture of all things is in us*

B2-C40-R07: Respect: We have a common culture. I am a cain stewar
from Bali. We just nee to respect each other, for the culture of all thin s is
represente in each human ein .

B2-C40-F15: Friendliness: Be a good listener. ,Are there times when a
 uest others you or asks stran e questions¡ " On a worl cruise it is ifferent, ecause we et to know the uest, an we are wi th them for four months.
They on't other us, ut they share their o o an a situations. They
mi ht share what happene on the shore that ay. My uests now like to
share all their cruise experiences, an I really like to listen.

B2-C40-L08: Leadership: Like a big University, cultures are teachers. , Do
you like all the ifferent cultures aoar the ship¡ " We learn from each other.

B2-C40-G05: Guests: Be a guest to learn how it feels. , I'm curious, when
you hear aout the customs of other places to se e, what it's like where they
live, woul you love to o visit them¡ " I have a frien livin in Darwin, so we
met in the city an ha a oo time seein each other.

B2-C40-F16: Friendliness: Stretch the circle of friends. , When you have lunch or meal times, o you always sit with someone from Bali¡ " Some from Myanmar an some others. From what I see, most people like to share with other nationalities.

B2-C40-D03: Development: People mature. Being cool is hard to learn. , As crew memers you always protect an take care of each other¡ " Yes, ut sometimes there is an er or a wor s sai , an the ship has zero tolerance for that type of ehavior. I have learne , as I et ol er, just to cool own.

CHAPTER FORTY-ONE: HK Jolly: *Happiness is contagious*

B2-C41-D04: Development: People grow from the values of parents. The frien liness comes with how you choose your frien s. If you rew up with oo frien s, nei hors an society, then you will e the same on oar e- cause you live here.

B2-C41-T06: Team/Family: Prolem solvers . The passen ers pass y where we are workin . So, we have to e always smilin . There are ups an   owns in our family as well. It"s like we have to collaorate with each other. Each an every prolem nee s to e solve . It's the same thin o ver here.

B2-C41-T07: Team/Family: There are no secrets in a team/family, only the joy of companionship. We are as a family. You have to stay to ether an live to ether. We share a same mess room, the crew memers, an everythin . We eat to ether, we make jokes, we make fun. A lot of times, we share with each other the sa ness an   oo times an the est ays. I norin someone is like killin someone's life an happiness. For me, I"ll just ive my est, an with a smile, even if I"m scare , I"m not showin it to anyone. A etter smile is a et- ter ay. I think so in my life.

B2-C41-L09: Lea ership: Quality leadership is contagious. I like to focus on people who are ivin a oo example for this worl . Happiness is conta- ious. If you are not happy, that means you are makin a mistake in your life. Whatever the sa ness is, the oo an the a come like the ti e in the water. You cannot expect the ti e will e just at that level, so sometimes it will e hi her. Sometimes we can have a isaster in one villa e so you have to always e prepare for this kin of a thin , oth lower an hi h ti es.

B2-C41-O05: Openin   up: People have to open up to let the truth in. I fol- low all cultures an all the reli ions. I try everyo y"s kin of foo , whatever it is. If I on't like it, I on't eat it.

B2-C41-i06: Incentives: Why would anyone wish to work 24-7? Who has money to see the worl ¡ Even if you trie to walk aroun the worl you woul never finish it. You cannot keep your ol footprints on all parts of the worl , you know. We just work for it.

B2-C41-C05: Creativity: The mind of an owner is creative. Whenever you work for the company, you have to e a very responsile person to rin this company up with ri htness. You know, this company will row much etter. We have to ive solutions; we have to ive our i eas. The company shoul have oo i eas, e cause we come from ifferent coun-tries. We on't nee to make a copy an paste from other companies. My mother always use to say, *"Don't follow the guy who is going the other way"*. You choose your way, which is etter for you.

B2-C41-W07: Workers: Workers could recruit others if asked. There are many people in my country waitin for a small jo on the ship or any-where else, ecause they nee lea ers like us to e ale to rin them alon .

B2-C41-D05: Development: Personal development can e encouraged with this kind of thinking. I wante to su est it. You know I am there for the crew after meetin s I o to. I represent them. I o for the safety meet-in , so I ive my su estions for them an pass it to the company. I'm reamin not only ao ut myself in the picture, ut I'm reamin for who look out for the jo. So, if we helpe this company in a etter way, the et-ter the future will ecome.

B2-C41-C06: Creativity: Workers can think simply or deeply. He reflects a culture of inclusion that's hard to maintain, ut it's happening. I'm very happy with this company. If there are 600 crew memers here, they were joless at home. Now they"re taken y the this employer. I am very prou for this owner. He was just like a crew memer. This owner, he has a i vi-sion. When we are orn, we come with zero sense. Everythin comes from our mother an father. Once we start learnin , that is our first step. When I first met the owner, he was like a crew memer, very frien ly. All of the osses are frien ly an helpful, askin questions an what are the pro-lems. I feel like I am at home here.

CHAPTER FORTY-TWO: Lighting/Sound Technician: *Frosting on performance cake*

B2-C42-J08: Joy: Workers exude their joy in various ways. My boss is the cruise director in the entertainment department. When I first came, I wanted to see different people, like different races. I see the world is like the cultural diversity on the ship. When you're on the ship, everybody thinks you speak English very well. On the ship, you can see different kinds of people, and you can see the world.

CHAPTER FORTY-THREE: Head Pastry Chef: *CMV gives freedom to grow*

B2-C43-C07: Creativity: Creativity is good for ot h crew and ship. This jo lets you express yourself. Ima ination is what comes to my min . I can create anythin at the moment. Noo y ju es you; you can use your own i eas. We o have the company's stan ar recipes. We have to follow those. But, when we have some uffets, you can use your own ima ination.

B2-C43-C08: Creativity: Creativity is unlimited with food. I'm in the foo in ustry; I really enjoy the foo from ifferent nationalities, especially Ukraine, Russia, In onesia, an I also enjoy the people an the frien ly ami-ance. It's really very nice. I min le less with my own nationality. I look for other nationalities.

B2-C43-D06: Development: Personal development is typical of crew. What o you think you've learne from workin on the ship¡ I i learn a lot. Goo an a , to e unselfish as well. That's the first thin , I think, ecause I was-n't like this when I first joine the ship.

B2-C43-D07 Development: Give and take. Better to give. What o you mean y ein unselfish¡ Peop le are just sometimes crew memers. It's a ive an take policy. If you ive your oo , the ay you stop, you want; it's like that. You've learne to e unselfish. I wasn't like this efore. I've learne a lot that is interestin .

B2-C43-K07: Kin ness: Winning y losing. , What o you think your secret is in ettin alon so well with people¡ " I think it's my kin ness. I'm a type of person to ive away thin s. I have a i heart. My assistants love workin with me. They miss me when they're on the other ships.

B2-C43-T08: Team/Family: The home feeling is another way to express in-clusion. I have never felt our ships were like a cruise liner; I just feel when I'm comin ack, it's like home; then when I see the same uests, it's really eau-tiful. When they know you an you know them, it's like an attachment.

B2-C43-M12: Multi-Cultural: If there is no "outgroup" the cultures feel comfortale and the differences interesting. , Do you fin the customs of all these cultures har to eal with¡ " I have een on oar for so many ye ars

that I know which people like what, an how to eal with ifferent nationalities. It's no prolem at all. I just ju   e everyo y the same way. As lon
as they coul e oo with me, then I am oo with them.

B2-C43-E13: En lish: English and gestures are languages to learn and
have fun with. , An   estures from other cultures you just et use to¡"
Yes, we o it quite often. Like when you are in Jamaica, you alrea y know
some stuff. We even use them at home with frien s. It's silly, ut it ets
into your enes, I uess.

B2-C43-P04: Promotion: Extra effort and creativity pay off. Last year,
there was one uy who was very intereste in pastries. He use to come after hours an work with me, pickin up hints. He alrea y has een promote in the same contract. It was very touchin for me. He is a aker
now, an I can see that smile on his face, an he loves what he is oin . I
am prou of myself, an my assistant wants to e a pastry chef. So, it's
like someo y rou ht me up, so n ow I am oin my est to ri n someone else up.

CHAPTER FORTY-FOUR: Bartender-Coffee Barista: _Smile: it doesn't cost anything_

B2-C44-P05: Promotion: Work for an opportunity. The hospitality in-
 ustry is aout service. Everythin is international. I worke with another
company efore , a Spanish company, an I was learnin Spanish lan-
 ua e. Then I trie to et a jo on a loal cruise line, last year, on Colum-
us. I starte as an assistant arten er. I starte to learn more how to
stan out, ecause ifferent companies have ifferent r ules. Then I ot a
promotion from my supervisor. They recommen e me to e a ar man-
a er.

B2-C44-E14: En lish: World citizens. I have a lot of frien s here from
Ukraine. Also, from UK, In ia, Myanmar, Belarus, an some ancers from
Ukraine an a lot of other nationalities. The speakin is always ifferent,
ecause they have a ifferent culture, ifferent accent. It is nice to work
with a lot of nationalities. We know ifferent cultures, ifferent lan-
 ua es.

B2-C44-O06: Openin up: Creativity. Sometimes it mi ht soun like
they are speakin ru ely, or they think I am not speakin well. But it's
not true, it's just the ifference in the lan ua e. We will un erstan how
they mana e, how they live in their home, in their country, ecause we
will see an example. It's how to work, how to live. Examples are Seria or

Ukraine. When we have een on oar a while, they will e talkin aout each an coconut, an I say to them that I have a lot of each an a lot of co-conut, so we will talk aout our cities. This i s ifferent, ut it makes us happy. We know a lot of kin s of foo , so from In onesia, or Ukraine, there is always ifferent foo .

B2-C44-G06: Guests: Creativity For me, smilin is like my personality. If you are an ry or hurt, you shoul never show to the outsi e. The thin is to smile; it oesn't cost anythin . No matter how ru e the passen er, how com-plainin the passen er, we serve with a smile. They will calm own, an they will e very happy.

B2-C44-C09: Creativity: Creativity with presentation. This is not special foo we serve here, ut if we serve with special service an with a smile, with our heart, they think it is special. If we on't have passen ers, then we on't have a jo. So, we nee to ive them the est service, so they will come ack a ain.

CHAPTER FORTY-FIVE: Bar Waiter: *I had three dreams*

B2-C45-M13: Multi-Cultural: Differences sound like fun. Identical is or-ing. , Do you think there are a vanta es to the cultural iversity on the ship¡" Everyo y's ifferent. This has helpe me un erstan a lot aout the people from Ukraine, Hon uras or In ia. It epen s also on the country. They're havin a ifferent kin of foo . I was tryin , most of them, the In-ian, the Hon uras, the Ukrainian; it's almost similar with mine. I think it ets pretty nice to meet other people from another country. That is, they are oin to open your min more.

B2-C45-H04: Heart/Hu s/Haits: Warm talk eats the internet. Maye I'm oin to have a new conversation, an I like to speak with the people. I learn a lot of thin s from the passen ers, from the places where they come from.

B2-C45-D08: Development: Mature workers rememer people, not things. I woul like to travel also, when I'm at the proper a e for my ki s. Because some people, for example, in my country, they're workin their entire life to have one, two cars, two houses, one apartment, ut actually they on't fin their happiness there. The people comin on the ship are happy. They visit a lot of places. That's a very mature attitu e. It really helps. But to e honest, on the ship, it's really nice to meet another kin of person.

B2-C45-O07: Openin up: 'Hello' is friendly. I want to know how to say hello in his lan ua e or thank you. It makes him happy that he is here, an these people that know my lan ua e are nice. It makes us oth com- fortale.

B2-C45-O08: Openin up: Honor their religion; learn something. I was havin a conversation with a uy. I am very intereste aout the o s from Hin u reli ion. Some of them involve the elephants. I'm a reli ious person, ut when it''s aout the reli ion, I'm very curious, ecause my ui e tol me aout each culture ha vin a o . I sai , just on't feel a that I am askin so many questions, ecause I just want to know more. When my collea ues ask me aout my c ountry, I just o on aout this an that. Come to visit me.

B2-C45-F17: Frien liness: Show an interest. Then for example, on my previous ship, they were havin an elephant statue, an each memer from the restaurant was lau hin an   ancin , an I aske what oes that mean. It was somethin aout the temple, an someone was explainin aout the culture, an that was very interestin . My collea ue just tol me the Water Festival is comin up as well as the Color Festival in In ia. He showe me some won erful pictures. So, I ha questions like why is that festival aout colors¡ I am open to this kin of knowle e.

B2-C45-D09: Development: Lifetime education makes you interesting. We have to know each other. An you have to know aout the reli ions, aout t he festivals, or what is the most visite place in a country. An why not¡ On my vacation, I am oin to visit.

CHAPTER FORTY-SIX: Home Office-Development: *All jobs are important*

B2-C46-R08: Respect: Respect and inclusion work everywhere. Jako's vi- sion ali ns with all mana ement people in implementin an attitu e of re- spect, teamwork, an carin for every team memer.

B2-C46-T09: Team/Family: Close support. These ays, there is also a theme that involves how to treat people, how to respect each other, an how to work with a multicultural team. He explains how mana ement supports them, an how each can support each other.

B2-C46-M14: Multi-Cultural: Leaders think: It's a won erful thin to have a multi-cultural, multi-nationality, multi-character firm. The lan ua e is En lish. The uys in the en ine room know that without servin foo an cleanin the cains, our four en ines own elow are useless. We woul not e sailin any more. The reverse is true on the hotel si e. This is the first thin , that we tell them: listen, all these jos on oar are important. This is from our mana ement point of view; I think that the clue is to ive all of our crew memers the feel in that they're important, from the person who is o-in the en ine control to the one who makes the e s.

B2-C46-C10: Creativity: Creativity involves a celeration of the Indian National Day. Different nationalities have invite their frien s from Belarus an elsewhere. Maye it"s ifferent reli ions, ifferent cultures, ifferent po-litical orientations, an   ifferent nationalities. If you o to the crew area, people are sittin an talkin to ether at the In onesians' tale for lunch or inner, for example, an also sittin with their community, ecause it"s easier for them to communicate.

<u>CHAPTER FORTY-SEVEN: Crew Ambassador: *Nothing is impossible*</u>

B2-C47-C11: Creativity: Entertaining crew: *"Happy crew makes happy guests."* What I do in a nutshell is exactly what a cruise ship director does for his passengers.

B2-C47-T10: Team/Family: Welcome: You are included. "You get an idea that even though you are of a different nationality, you are going to be wel-comed?" The majority of people, when you ask what would you prefer, 1) to work in a diverse environment or 2) would you rather work with a majority of one nationality, would choose #1. I believe 99% would say they want to work in a diverse environment.

B2-C47-E15: English: Goldilocks numbers needed. The problem is, when you have a majority country, the drawback is, many wouldn't use English as their main language for communication, and that is not good for us because we are here for the guests. The guest is the bread and butter. We need to be diverse. We suggest: "You don't get better in English if you don't use it."

<u>CHAPTER FORTY-EIGHT: Crew Ambassador: *The more you give, the more you get*</u>

B2-C48-M15: Multi-Cultural: The crew is happy with the food. We have to keep in mind the different nationalities. There might be something you like. If you don't eat pork, there will be something else. There will be something if I'm a vegetarian. If they don't like something, or it's not tasting nice, they can tell me, and I can speak to the chef.

B2-C48-P06: Promotion: Promotions go to those who care. I try to tell them, get experience. I started in 2006 from the smallest position, because in

India, no matter what experience you have, you need to start from the lowest. I started to be a galley cleaner, but in two years over there, I got one of the biggest promotions. One minute, I was a person cleaning the galley, and in the next contract, I'm sitting right next to the captain.

B2-C48-P07: Promotion: Creativity I always tell them to work hard; the company's growing, and you can grow. I'm a living example for you. I was in the restaurant with some of you guys. If you want to grow, just do your best.

B2-C48-D10: Development: Maturity requires perspective. That's how you motivate them; they're going to stay on the same page. It's not always blue skies. Sometimes it's going to rain, sometimes sunny. You have to take it the way it comes.

B2-C48-E16: English: Speak to learn. I always tell them try to speak in English, not their mother tongue. If you don't speak, you will never learn. You have to try, even if it's broken English. One crew member could understand English, but he spoke very broken English when he joined. I just saw him now a few months later, and he is speaking very good English.

B2-C48-E17: English: Try. I always say try; even if you are incorrect, someone will correct you, so you can learn. They might not actually speak, but they have to understand and use it for reports, because, in an emergency, that's the only language we use. Communication. It can change someone's life. . . . Just communicate; that's really important.

CHAPTER FORTY-NINE: Chef: *I learn more deeply from the ship*

B2-C49-M16: Multi-Cultural. Safety in many cultures. "Do you think that all of the different cultures on the ship have influenced you?" Of course. When I was in India, and I was 14, there were not too many nationalities. But here, I came on board, and I saw Romanian people, Ukrainians, and Indonesians. I came to know people that are friendly, interesting, and honest with us. It's all about our mentality. If you are good by heart, other people are good by heart. It doesn't matter which country, nothing. Good environment, good atmosphere.

B2-C49-H05: Heart/Hugs/Habits: Be yourself. Everybody should smile at each other, love each other. Try to try to forget the problems, worries, sadness, everything. I belong to a Hindu family. I am interested in the culture of the Hindus. We can say all Indians are Hindus, because it is not a religion. It's a culture. In India, all Muslims or Christians or Hindus belong to Hindu culture. "So that kind of warmth and friendliness is part of the Hindu religion?"

You can see all the books about India. You would not go forward making issue with other people, because the meaning of Hindu books is only one thing. Peace. If you read these books, you would not fight.

CHAPTER FIFTY: Head of Marketing: *Create a pleasing atmosphere*

B2-C50-T11: Team/Family: Teamwork. It is a tribute to top management that many of the interviewees have re-phrased in their own words the truism that without the success of each member of the team, the guests will not return for more of the top level of service and satisfaction that the workers strive to deliver.

B2-C50-S02: Supervision: The Plan. Put another way, the oal of every worker an the lea ers is to create an atmosphere that pleases every uest while keepin that pro uct affor ale, fun, an even excitin .

B2-C50-S03: Supervision: Good for crew, guests, and growth. The com- ine success of these efforts will create jos an promotion opportunities as the cruise line ecomes known an expan s its fleet. The tea m is responsile for the excellence of the pro uct. Marketin is responsile for informin the worl that it is availale an worth iscoverin .

CHAPTER FIFTY-ONE: Hotel Director: *Leadership: Strong empathy for crew*

B2-C51-C12: Creativity: Creativity The point here is that Elian and every person on the CMV team is empathetic to the new hire, and also the experi- enced crew member, and they organize ways to make their welcome work. They now have a Crew Ambassador who attends to the physical and mental challenges with hands-on help, including help in contacting family to assure them of his safe arrival.

B2-C51-C13: Creativity: Creativity Elian is justly proud of their returning crew numbers. We have an 82% record for joining crew returning; that's high in this industry. Normally the industry is about 70 or 72%, but that depends. The last year we just achieved 82%, from 80.15%; it's going up.

B2-C51-BO: Banking for cash pay: Wages paid in cash. We do some special things for our crew. Cash for wages is important, because some workers don't use banks. If you want, we can pay you in cash. Because, for example, people come in and say the bank system is so corrupt. I will accept the con- tract if I can get cash. We say, okay, we will do it. We have to deliver the cash.

Conclusions

Books 1 and 2 are for everyone. We share a planet with nature and our fellow citizens. We each have a curiosity about both that translates into studying human nature and biological and physical nature. Each of us has the freedom to live our lives as we choose. The stories of the crew members aboard a floating resort are heart-felt expressions of people serving people. In the process they have a job that makes it possible for them to support their families, make new friends, and fulfill their dreams. They discover that, although we each have different cultures, there is much to be learned from befriending those who are different in ways like gender, age, skin tones, religion, customs, religion, priorities, food preferences, language, lifestyles, and attitudes. If we can celebrate our friendships with folks that used to be in an "out group", excluded from our circle of communication, we have advanced in maturity, knowledge, and enrichment in our lives. And in addition, we are more likely to be successful in what we have chosen to do with our career and social life.

The crew members have learned that although they might have wished that everyone could be exactly like themselves, that is not realistic, so they learn to celebrate the differences. A traveler explores the world out of curiosity to see different ways to look at and do things. They also learn that teamwork is good for their career, makes for happy and cooperative successes, and is more fun than arguing about things that are not really important.

If nations could do as well, what a great planet this would be, with everyone being kind and helpful. So, draw your own conclusions from these dozens of stories. You are free to choose your attitudes, because no one else can make that choice. Which choice will make you and your loved ones happier, enhance your career and the success of your organization, and build better friendships?

The author of books 1 and 2 is a photo-journalist who has traveled and recorded images of people in villages, large and small, doing their daily activities and pleasing travelers who are open to experiencing new ideas and customs. Enjoy a vicarious trip with her, celebrate your opportunities at work and play that make life interesting, and share your new attitudes and your discovery of friends that are "different".

Our planet is full of interesting people and wonders of nature. Check out the author page for more adventures.

Part 6: Evaluation options and organizational "health" checkup

The potential for research may be irresistible to some employers. This is a very sensitive area that requires care in avoiding the suspicion that honest evaluations by workers might harm their future, so trustworthy industrial psychologists must have systems to get honest answers for the management without causing workers to become uncomfortable. There are always ways for a worker to waive that identity shroud and present improvement ideas, but for purposes of an organizational "wellness" evaluation, there are excellent and inexpensive survey methods available.

One professional organization (there may be others) has indicated they would be willing to customize a national standards wellness survey so as to capture, at the moment after a worker reads book 1 or 2, the state of mind before and after reading it. There will never be another opportunity to "un-ring" the bell, so this can be discussed with the publisher, who met one such firm at a SHRM D/I conference and would work with any firm wishing to consider this option.

Contact: *Publisher@inclusionPLUSdiversity.com*

Part 7: Free trial options: easy steps to achieve Inclusion results

This area is designed to help those employers and their H.R. staff who wish to be creative but at virtually no cost commitment and no risk of failure of the mission. There is a simple answer. Send the following information to the publisher to begin a dialog toward doing a test mailing to a few different co-horts of workers. Some variance involving high to low rank and income, plus some variables like gender, nationality, age, etc. would be helpful.

In the email, include the total number of licenses needed to test the feasibil-ity of a full mailing (up to something like 100 persons) and the total number that represents the entire work force, plus supply chain or consultants, doc-tors, independent contractors, or other workers if that might be desired.

Provide all contact information and what is the current program to address "inclusion" along with any known do or don't factors in that program.

If eBooks are to be licensed, the cost for eBooks would not exceed $2 per re-cipient, for the license, and if print copies are desired, the same amount would be added to either the delivered cost for a drop shipment, or to the to-tal run if the publisher supplied the masters for employer to provide to the printer. All are negotiable.

In some cases, there might be a charge for customization of the text of the eBook or print book, but generally there would be no charge for a license for the customer to translate the text to any language desired by the sponsor.

Other questions will be answered promptly.

This is intended as a supplement to any existing programs, but it has a strong potential for success, is inexpensive (a dollar or two per worker!), and can be completed within a week if the goal is to get the book to everyone about the same time. It has the potential to prevent misunderstandings, lan-guage confusion, disrespect leading to lost talents, and loss of creativity due to a lack of inclusion feelings on the part of some workers. It should also lead to information about how to "fix" misunderstandings in other areas that contained hidden problems.

We look forward to hearing from you. Publisher@inclusionPLUSdiver-sity.com

Part 8: Further reading in diversity and inclusion. [See Part 3 also]

For EVERY worker, these stories will celebrate inclusion and open minds:
"24-7: Multi-Cultural Workers Find Diversity Recipe to Heal a Troubled World"
Paperback – December 15, 2017 by <u>Jackie Chase</u> (Author) Available in eBook or
Paperback, color or grayscale from Amazon. Get volume bid quote from: <u>pub-</u>
<u>lisher@inclusionPLUSdiversity.com</u>

*The sequel is another 24-7 book which is an INCLUSION book about Crew Life
from another large employer in the hospitality industry that may be ordering
copies for its workers.*

HR Professional Books/Articles to Read:
The following books [and many more eBooks and print books] are
available at <u>www.bookshout.com</u>. Text is from each website for
convenience in shopping:

<u>https://www.bookshout.com/ebooks/</u>**building-on-the-promise-of-diversity   [2005] See web**

<u>https://www.bookshout.com/ebooks/</u>**change-the-culture-change-the-game 2011**

<u>https://www.bookshout.com/ebooks/</u>**cultivating-a-creative-culture**

<u>https://www.bookshout.com/ebooks/</u>**driven-by-difference**

<u>https://www.bookshout.com/ebooks/</u>**exclusion**

[<u>goo.gl/AvDmrA</u>   <<<Short URL for title above: *"10-must-reads..."*]

<u>https://www.bookshout.com/ebooks/</u>**leading-culture-change**

<u>https://www.bookshout.com/ebooks/</u>**overcoming-bias**

<u>https://www.bookshout.com/ebooks/</u>**permission-to-speak-freely**

<u>https://www.bookshout.com/ebooks/</u>**selling-women-short**--2

<u>https://www.bookshout.com/ebooks/</u>**the-diversity-bonus**

https://www.bookshout.com/ebooks/**the-millennial-myth**

https://www.bookshout.com/ebooks/**the-multicultural-mind**

https://www.bookshout.com/ebooks/**the-respectful-leader**--3

https://www.bookshout.com/ebooks/**the-xyz-factor**--2

https://www.bookshout.com/ebooks/**we-can-t-talk-about-that-at-work**

https://www.bookshout.com/ebooks/**why-should-anyone-work-here**

Appendix: Articles about Inclusion and Financial Advantages to Organizations:

https://hbr.org/2018/12/to-retain-employees-focus-on-inclusion-not-just-diversity
To Retain Employees, Focus on Inclusion — Not Just Diversity by Karen Brown, December 4, 2018

https://hbr.org/2018/04/how-to-lose-your-best-employees **How to Lose Your Best Employees by** Whitney Johnson, April 20, 2818
This article talks about the better way to lose a manager: which is to groom a talented, possibly a "hidden" or "minority, such as female, subordinate to take his place.

https://hbr.org/2018/06/to-retain-new-hires-make-sure-you-meet-with-them-in-their-first-week
To Retain New Hires, Make Sure You Meet with Them in Their First Week: Authors: Dawn Klinghoffer, Candice Young, Xue Liu June 14, 2018 UPDATED June 14, 2018

This article talks about first impressions and their importance for best use of talent.
Poor onboarding experiences can lead to unnecessary and preventable turnover, the cost of which can be as much as twice the employee's annual salary.
There are numerous articles about the financial and creative advantages of diversity in publications from McKinsey and the Harvard Business Review and elsewhere. The website will be kept up to date from time to time as new studies are published.

Author Page

It is true that armchair travelers [readers] can experience vicariously many of the same feelings that a talented author can convey. This author's books are pure fun and are written by a "mom" who is one of us, a reporter, not an anthropologist or scientist. Workers in any nation or organization can continue their quest to become a better-informed citizen of the world, reaching out to a foreign person with a smile and more, by continuing to read about this author's experiences abroad.

Jackie Chase, [JackieChase.com, WorldTravelDiva.com, and CulturesOfThe-World.com], has traveled to over 100 countries and specializes in staying in remote villages in order to use her keen observations and photo-journalism skills to share her insights with her reader fans. She has traveled alone, with a child, with family, and with friends; she has earned over 32 awards from international book contests from 2014 to date of printing; she shares with the public many of the travel secrets she has experienced in her book titled, ***"How to Become an Escape Artist" A Traveler's Handbook.*** The Handbook was tested for several years with students in a college evening class, and they soaked up Jackie's hints and the many ways to avoid disappointment, reduce expenses and frustrations, navigate the issues of visas, language, customs, currencies, accommodations, transportation, attitudes, danger, travel alone, and other problems all covered in over 190 segments in the book. It is up to date with nearly 100 click links to hard-to-find websites dealing with all aspects of travel, including finding companions.

Her ***"All Hands Working Together" Cruise for a Week: Meet 79 Cultures*** book treats cruising in a unique way to learn about cultures; the reader experiences personal contact with crewmembers from many of the 79 countries they represent, and from many skills they possess.

Jackie Chase has written definitive books on "People to Meet" in contrast to "Places to See". She convinces her readership to look beyond mountains, lakes and buildings to see world inhabitants of all continents as potential friends and shows how much we have in common. She shows how to bridge gaps created by custom and language in ***"100 People to Meet before You Die: Travel to Exotic Places"***. This book, [as well as the others], are available in color, grayscale, and, with stunning images in eBooks that come to life on backlit screens. This anthology involves 12 countries and contains 321 of those story-telling images and award-winning prose about her adventures. For her fans of a particular country, she has twelve "singles" in print and in eBook format, plus at least one (Panama) translated into Spanish.

For children, from small up through teens, a "winner" of a book is *"Giraffe-Neck Girl" Make Friends with Different Cultures*. It is about a ten-year-old girl in Thailand who warms the hearts of young and old as she shares her different life and customs.

Jackie Chase's 2016 book, *"Walking to Woot" A Photographic Narrative Discovering New Dimensions for Parent-Teen Bonding* has won 17 international awards in the genres of Parenting, Young Adult Non-fiction, Multi-Cultural, Cover Design and Travel, and it contains both poetic descriptions and visual ones with its nearly 170 images of life with stone-age tribal warriors who haven't changed customs in a thousand years. The New Guinea unclothed villagers welcomed Jackie and her blond 14-year-old daughter to pig roasts, unusual customs, and dances. Jackie Chase loves to hear from her fans and to see copies of reviews they submit to the web. Contact her at:
JakartaMoon@hotmail.com

BOOKS BY JACKIE CHASE: 2014/16
How to Become an Escape Artist: A Traveler's Handbook (2014-6)
Giraffe-Neck Girl: Make Friends with a Different Culture (2014)
100 People to Meet before You Die: Travel to Exotic Cultures (2014-6)

AWARDS (15) FOR THE FOUR BOOKS LISTED ABOVE
Royal Palm Literary Award; National Indie Excellence Book Award; FAPA President's Book Award; Readers' Favorite Book Award; International Book Award; USA Best Book Award; Beverly Hills Book Awards

AWARDS (17) For: *"Walking to Woot"* A Photographic Narrative Discovering New Dimensions for Parent-Teen Bonding:
Beach Book: & San Francisco: Festivals; Beverly Hills Book Award in 3 Genres; Eric Hoffer Grand Prize Award in 2 Genres; Florida Authors and Publishers Association (FAPA, including cover award); International Book Award, Montaigne Medals; National Indie Excellence Award; Next Generation Indie Book Award in 2 Genres; Paris Book: Festival; Reader's Favorite Award in 3 Genres.

BUSINESS BOOKS BY JACKIE CHASE: 2017 and 2019 (This one)
'24-7' Multi-Cultural Workers Find Diversity Recipe to Heal a Troubled World
[Sharing inclusion/diversity ideas with employees/students/managers in businesses, charities and governments using inexpensive eBook distribution methods to reach every participant in the organization].

For further information, see www.inclusionPLUSdiversity.com

www.ingramcontent.com/pod-product-compliance
Lightning Source LLC
Chambersburg PA
CBHW061834220326
41599CB00027B/5281